Super Sleepover Guide

Look for these and other books
in the Sleepover Friends Series:

Super Sleepover Guide

Susan Saunders

AN
APPLE
PAPERBACK

SCHOLASTIC INC.
New York Toronto London Auckland Sydney

ISBN 0-590-42662-1

12 11 10 9 8 7 6 5 4 3 2 1   9/8 0 1 2 3 4/9

Printed in the U.S.A.   28

First Scholastic printing, August 1989

CONTENTS

Chapter 1
We Love Sleepovers!

I love sleepovers! And I — I'm Lauren Hunter — have been to more sleepovers than anyone else I know. Anyone, that is, except my friend Kate Beekman! Kate and I and our friends Stephanie Green and Patti Jenkins are the Sleepover Friends. Every Friday night we get together for a sleepover. Sometimes we play Truth or Dare, sometimes we watch movies, sometimes we even go out of town to have our sleepover. And we *always* have great munchies.

1

Why We Decided to Write a Sleepover Guide

Lately, a lot of kids in our fifth grade class, Mrs. Mead's 5B at Riverhurst Elementary School, have been asking us for advice on how they can throw their own super sleepovers. And so have a lot of people like you, people who have read all about our adventures in the *Sleepover Friends* series.

I guess everyone has been asking us for help because we are sleepover *experts*. We have had some of the best sleepovers and some of the most disastrous sleepovers ever! We have learned the hard way what to do to make a sleepover lots of fun. So we decided to write *The Sleepover Friends' Super Sleepover Guide*. (Patti, who is one of the smartest kids in the fifth grade, thought of the name. *Stephanie*) Everything you need to know to throw a great sleepover is in this book. And once you've tried our ideas, we hope you'll think of many more ways to make a sleepover terrific — and tell us all about them.

We love sleepovers (That's why we have one almost every Friday night! *Patti*), and we're sure that you will love them, too!

When to Have a Sleepover

There are lots of great times to have sleep-overs. In fact, almost any night except a school night is perfect. We started having our sleepovers on Fridays during the school year because we couldn't wait for Saturday. Now they are a year-round Friday-night tradition.

It's especially fun to have a sleepover on a special occasion, like your birthday or a holi-day. In our opinion, though, there really aren't enough holidays in the year. Fortunately, we have a solution for that problem. When there are no holidays or special occasions coming up, invent your own!

If you want to plan a holiday or a made-up occasion sleepover, try one of our favorites:

Special Occasion Sleepovers

• *Birthdays.* The number one sleepover oc-casion! Surprise birthday sleepovers that you throw for a friend are fun, too.

• *Fourth of July.* Start the party at your local fireworks display. Pack a picnic dinner for your guests. Then head back to your house for an all-American sleepover pillow fight.

• *Halloween*. Do you like ghosts, witches, and scary stories? Share them with your friends! Have everyone meet at your house to get into costume for neighborhood trick-or-treating. Return to your house to eat your treats and tell ghost stories late into the night!

• *School Holiday*. Those days when school is called off because our teacher has to go to a meeting are real holidays to us. Help your friends celebrate their unexpected freedom.

• *End of School*. Celebrate the first day of summer vacation with a stay-up-late, sleep-in sleepover!

Some of Our Favorite Made-Up Occasions

• *International Night*. Do you dream of exotic places? Go international by dressing in clothes from one country, eating foods from another, and playing games from a third! Travel around the world overnight!

• *Make your own sundaes*. Food is one of my favorite occasions, especially dessert. Supply your friends with different kinds of ice cream, syrups, nuts, whipped cream, sprinkles, bananas, and strawberries. Make the heavenly sundae of your dreams.

4

• *Rock Video Night.* Watch videos, and then direct your own! Lip-sync to your favorite song. (I would if I could get the microphone away from Stephanie! *Kate*) Go crazy on the air guitar. If you have access to a video camera, tape your performance and then play it back . . . if you dare!

• *Cheer Up a Friend Night.* Got a friend who's feeling down? Nothing will cheer her up faster than a special sleepover where she is the star for the night. Stephanie, Kate, and I once threw a sleepover for Patti when she got a bad grade on a math test. (Like a B. *Stephanie*) It worked like a charm. Patti felt much better and even got an A on her next test.

• *Arts and Crafts Night.* Plan a project that you and your friends can work on together. Make friendship bracelets with bright embroidery floss or use tempera paint and a long piece of craft paper to paint a mural for your room or your friend's.

• *Any-day Sleepover.* Invite your friends over for no reason at all except to have a good time!

Before You Have a Sleepover

Having a sleepover, especially a super sleepover, takes a lot of planning. After you decide to throw a sleepover party, think about these things before you announce your plans:

• *Do I have my parents' OK?* Never plan a sleepover without first getting your parents' permission. Here are some things to talk over with your parents:

Bedtime. Your parents will probably allow you to stay up later than usual for a special event like a sleepover, but make sure to ask them first. Remember that the rest of your family will want to sleep even if you and your guests are awake. It is very important to not be too noisy. For example, Kate's father is a doctor, so sometimes he works strange hours and is tired early in the evening. We always try extra hard to be quiet when we are at Kate's house.

Number of guests. Ask your parents how many people you are allowed to invite — before you begin inviting.

Budget. Ask your parents how much money you can spend. Mostly, you will need money for food, but don't forget about invitations, prizes, etc.

Ground rules. Does your family have any special rules of the house that your friends should know about? Every family has its own rules, so those you take for granted may be unfamiliar to your friends. For instance, at Stephanie's the living room is the busiest room in the house, but at Kate's house it's for adults only. Make sure that you tell your guests the rules *before* a disaster happens.

• *What kind of refreshments should I serve?* We always have plenty to eat at our sleepovers, and we have tons of suggestions for food that you can serve. Keep your budget in mind, and don't forget breakfast! If you don't have much money to spend, you may have to decide between having five friends over for a cookout, or twelve for chips and soda. Another thing that can be fun and inexpensive is to ask each one of your guests to bring something to share. If you do this, be sure to suggest something for each guest to bring. Otherwise, you may end up with eight bowls of dip and no chips for dipping!

• *Where will we sleep?* If your bedroom is large, it is the best place, since you will have the most privacy there. If you are going to have more than a few friends, you are probably going to have to move into the den or living room. If it is warm outside, move into the backyard instead!

• *How can I make my sleepover the best?* Plan ahead. The thing we like most about sleepovers is that something totally unexpected — and lots of fun — always happens. We're sure you'll feel the same way. Still, you should plan some activities, just to get the evening started. We have lots of suggestions for you in Chapters 2 through 6.

Help your guests be prepared, too. Send your guests a checklist of things to bring to a sleepover. It is one way that you can make sure your guests bring everything that they need. (And leave with everything, too! *Patti*).

The checklist we use is on the next page.

Sleepover Friends Sleepover Checklist

Sleepovers are much more fun when you have everything you need to be comfortable and to feel at home. Check each item off before you go to the party and before you go home. Make sure to label things that could get mixed up with other guests' belongings!

Packed	Took Home	
_____	_____	Sleep gear: pajamas or night-shirt, socks or slippers
_____	_____	Clothes for the morning
_____	_____	Toothbrush
_____	_____	Comb or brush
_____	_____	Washcloth and towel
_____	_____	Sleeping bag (or blanket and sheet bedroll) and pillow
_____	_____	Other _____

We left the last space blank, in case you want to add something to our list.

Try to plan ahead for things that could go wrong. For example — a monster invasion! Kate's sister Melissa (better known as Melissa the Monster! *Kate*) loves to crash our sleepovers. The solution is distraction. Ask your mom or dad to help you out if you don't want your little brother or sister involved in your party. Or maybe they could sleep over at a friend's for the evening. Or offer to take them out before the sleepover to rent their favorite videos for the night, or make a special sibling snack tray with a few of your refreshments, so they will feel like the night is special for them, too.

• *How do I invite people?* Written invitations are always a good idea. That way, no one forgets any important details — like the time and day of the party — and you don't forget to invite someone. Your invitation will tell your guests what kind of party to expect. A simple note means a casual party. A fancy card engraved in silver means a fancy affair. (That's what I'm using for my sweet sixteen sleepover in a few years. *Stephanie*) If your party has a theme, your invitations should fit it. If you throw one of our theme parties you can use the drawings in Chapter 7 to help, or you can just look at them to help you with your own ideas.

A sleepover invitation should always include:

- Date and time to come
- Time guests should leave the next day
- Your address and phone number
- The occasion, if there is one
- Things to bring (You can use the checklist on page 9.)

That's it! Now that you have picked a date, talked to your parents, decided on an occasion, and done everything else we described in this chapter, you are ready to have a good sleepover party.

But you want to have a *great* party, right? Well, that's why we didn't end this book right here. Keep reading to find out how to turn a so-so sleepover into a super one!

Chapter 2
Fun and Food
for a Fabulous Sleepover

Question: What are the fifteen most boring words in the world?
Answer: What do you want to do?
I don't know. What do you want to do?

If that sounds familiar, don't worry. We know tons of fabulous things to do at a sleepover. (And fabulous things to eat, too! *Patti*). All you have to do is keep reading, and you'll become a sleepover expert, too!

12

Games

To get started, here are some of our favorite sleepover games, guaranteed to get your party off to a terrific start. (But fun anytime, really. *Kate*)

• *Truth or Dare.* Our all-time favorite! The rules are simple, but the results are exciting! Decide who will go first. The first player picks her victim and asks THE question: Truth or Dare? If the victim chooses Truth, then the first player asks her any question she likes. (Our favorites: "Who is the cutest boy in school?" and "Would you rather spend an entire day with Angela Kemp, the nastiest girl in our class, or kiss Robert Ellwanger, the nerdiest boy?" *Stephanie*) The answerer must respond truthfully. If she refuses to answer, or if she chooses Dare to begin (probably because she is afraid to pick Truth! *Kate*), then she has to do whatever you dare her to do. A good dare is slightly embarrassing or hard to do, like singing the "Star-Spangled Banner" in the front yard, or rubbing your stomach and your head at the same time. An impossible dare, like holding your breath for ten minutes, is not fair and not allowed. (They always make me call up Robert Ellwanger and ask him to the movies!

Stephanie) When the victim has answered a question or finished a dare, she chooses the next victim. (That's why you should never ask anyone to do anything *too* awful for a dare or ask them anything too embarrassing for a truth: They may get you back when it's their turn! *Kate*)

• *Silly Stories.* Before your friends arrive, pick a short passage from a book or magazine. Then rewrite it, replacing some of the nouns, verbs, and adjectives with blanks. Under the blanks, write *noun, verb,* or *adjective,* so that you remember what part of speech belongs there. At the party — without reading your friends the passage — ask them for words that are the correct part of speech, and then write the words in the blanks. When you have filled in all the spaces, read the passage with the new words. It will sound very silly!

• *Telephone.* For this game, the more people, the better. Sit in a circle. Choose someone to go first. The first person thinks of a simple sentence or two, then whispers it into the ear of the person sitting next to her. That person then repeats what she has heard to the person sitting next to her, and so on around the circle. The last person announces what she heard whispered into her ear to the whole group. The first speaker then reveals what she said at the beginning of the game. The difference will be amazing and amusing. You can play again and again until everyone has had a chance to start it off. Last time we played, "I like brownies with ice cream" turned into "Select clowns with extra feet"!

• *Jumble.* I love this game! (That's because she is so tall and limber that she always wins. *Kate*, *Patti*, and *Stephanie*)

You'll need several pieces of construction paper in four different colors, dice, a bowl, note paper, a pencil, clear tape, scissors, and an old sheet (ask first!) or a smooth floor.

To get ready, cut the construction paper into large squares. Tape the squares to the sheet or floor so that they form a rough rectangle, with a space of about six inches between each piece of paper. Tape a tiny piece of each color of construction paper to the sides of a die. You'll only need to use four out of the six sides, so you may want to repeat two of the colors. Using the note paper and tape, label the second die on all six sides: L foot, L hand, L elbow, R hand, R foot, R knee. (R = right, L = left.)

To play, pick a person to roll the dice and

call out the results: Right hand, red, for example. All the players must put that part of her body on the right color. If you lose your balance, you're out. The last player left standing wins the game.

• *Who Am I?* Pin the name of someone famous, or at least famous with your friends, on each of your guests' backs, without letting anyone see who she's getting. Players take turns asking yes or no questions to try and guess their own identities. The first player to guess who she is wins. We like to play until everyone has guessed correctly.

• *Board Games.* Great for a small group. Monopoly, Pictionary, Risk, Scrabble, Clue, Jeopardy, Trivial Pursuit, Boggle, whatever you have in your closet! Especially fun on a stormy night with hot chocolate and popcorn.

Food

The Sleepover Friends have spent a lot of time testing sleepover foods. (That is an understatement! *Kate*) We've decided that the best recipes are the ones that taste yummy and are easy and fun to make and eat. Here are some of our all-time favorites:

The Main Course

If you invite your guests to come over early in the evening, you'll probably want to serve them dinner at your house. Your invitations should say if you *are* serving a meal.

Dinner will be more fun if you pick a main dish that everyone can help make. This is a great sleepover recipe because your guests can pick their own toppings and get just what they like.

Personal Pizza

1 English muffin for each guest
1 jar prepared tomato spaghetti sauce (15 oz)
½ lb mozzarella cheese, grated
Parmesan cheese
Toppings: pepperoni, mushrooms, green
    pepper; try anything!

Before your guests arrive, prepare toppings by cutting them into bite-sized pieces, and pre-heat the oven to 425 degrees. When you're ready to eat, split the English muffins in half. Spoon on enough spaghetti sauce to cover the muffin. Let your guests add their own toppings. Cover with mozzarella and a pinch of Parmesan. Place on a cookie sheet and bake for 15 minutes.

Salad or Snack

I have to admit that I am pretty lucky. I can eat cookies, cakes, and candies without gaining any weight. Actually, it isn't just luck — I jog with my brother, Roger, three or four times a week. Also, I love to eat fruits and vegetables almost as much as sweets. This fruit salad is one of my favorites.

Rainbow Fruit Salad

You can put any kind of fruit into a fruit salad — I usually use my favorite, or whatever is in season, or what is in the fridge. This fruit salad is special because everything in it is a different color.

Choose one fruit from each category:

Red: watermelon, fresh strawberries, raspberries
Orange: cantaloupe, oranges
Green: honeydew melon, green grapes, kiwis, Granny Smith apples
Yellow: bananas, grapefruit
Purple: plums, purple grapes
Blue: blueberries

You'll need about two cups of each kind of fruit, but sometimes when you are buying fruit it is hard to judge. Don't worry — it is okay to put more in. Rinse the fruit and cut into bite-sized pieces. If you have picked a lot of sour fruit (like Granny Smith apples, raspberries, or grapefruit) and you would like the salad sweeter, you can stir in ½ cup of sugar (granulated or confectioners') or honey.

Dessert

This dessert on the next page is our favorite because it's elegant enough for any occasion, but simple enough to make any time. And you assemble each serving separately, so that you don't make too much or too little. Just make sure to save some for a post-sleepover pick-me-up when your friends have gone home, and you've got to clean the family room all by yourself!

Strawberry Shortcake

1 medium-sized store-bought pound cake
1 pint fresh strawberries
EITHER 1 pint heavy cream, 1 tablespoon
   powdered sugar, and vanilla extract for
   homemade whipped cream
OR 1 can prepared whipped cream

    To make homemade whipped cream, pour refrigerated cream into a mixing bowl and beat it. It is done when you can lift up the beater and the cream forms peaks. (This will take a few minutes, but it is worth it, so don't give up! *Patti*) Add a few drops of vanilla extract and about a tablespoon of powdered sugar. Beat again until well mixed. Take the stems off of the strawberries, rinse, and slice them. Slice the cake into pieces about an inch thick and place the slices on a plate. Cover with strawberries and whipped cream. Makes 8 to 10 servings.

Drinks

Don't forget something to drink. Soda is definitely the easiest, but it can be expensive for a big party. It is cheaper to make fruit punch or lemonade. You can buy mixes for these at the supermarket. Of course, on a cold winter night, hot chocolate is great, but nothing beats my hot apple cider. (I love it when Lauren makes this because the whole house smells cozy. *Patti*) This is perfect for a winter sleepover.

Hot Apple Cider

½ gallon apple cider for every 8 guests
cinnamon sticks

The only hard thing about this recipe is making sure that you buy the right things. Apple juice isn't any good. It has to be "brown" apple cider. And make sure that you get cinnamon sticks, not ground cinnamon. Put the cider in a pan, add three or four cinnamon sticks, and heat over a low flame. When the cider is hot, remove the cinnamon and pour into mugs. Put one fresh stick of cinnamon in each mug.

Breakfast

Most of your sleepover fun will go on in the evening , but your guests will still be there in the morning. So don't forget breakfast! You may not want to keep things as simple as cold cereal, milk, juice, and fruit. Maybe one of your parents has a breakfast specialty that they would be willing to make. If you want things to be extra special, try our favorite breakfast recipe, blueberry pancakes. (This recipe is perfect for turning frowns upside down when everyone's cranky from not getting enough sleep! *Kate*)

Blueberry Pancakes

pancake mix
blueberries
oil (for frying)

Make the pancake batter according to the directions on the box. (You may need eggs, water, or oil — read the box before you leave the market and make sure to get everything you need.) Add about 1 cup of blueberries for every 4 cups of batter, more if you like your pancakes very berry.

(It's better if you guess — trying to measure exactly will make you crazy. *Stephanie*) If you are using canned blueberries, drain them first. If you can't get blueberries, try sliced strawberries, sliced bananas, sliced apples, or even fruit salad left over from the night before!

Follow the directions on the package for cooking. Or, for extra fun, try these cooking variations:

Initial Pancakes. Pour batter from a spoon onto a hot griddle to make the shape of an initial. Draw the letter backwards so it will look right when you flip the pancake out of the pan. (You may want to practice!) When the letter is firm around the edges, pour enough batter into the pan to cover it. Finish cooking normally.

Animal Pancakes. Pour batter for body shape into the pan. Trickle small amounts of batter around the body for head, ears, legs, and a tail.

Silver Dollar Pancakes. Pour one tablespoon of batter into pan for each pancake. Keep pancakes as round and even as possible. Pile up high and spear with a decorated toothpick.

Serve your pancake creations with butter and syrup or powdered sugar.

Planning a sleepover is easier if you are organized. There is a lot to do — inviting, planning, shopping, cooking — so I always use the chart on the next page. I'm sure that it will help you, too!

Now you know the basics! You are ready to throw a super sleepover, but we experts still have some secrets up our sleeves! In the following chapters, we'll each show you step-by-step how to put together a sleepover we've tried and loved.

Super Planning Chart

Four weeks before:
  Talk to your parents about
    Permission
    Ground rules
    Budget
    Number of guests
  Pick a date
  Choose a theme

Three weeks before:
  Decide on refreshments
  Choose activities and games

Two weeks before:
  Decide on guest list
  Prepare and send out invitations

One week before:
  Make sure that you know who is coming
  Buy supplies for decorations and activities

The day before:
  Buy food
  Clean your room
  Put up decorations, if you are having any

The day of the Super Sleepover:
  Relax and get ready to have a great time!

Chapter 3
Stephanie's Supernatural Sleepover

Hi. I'm Stephanie Green. Like all the Sleepover Friends, I love any kind of sleepover. But my all-time favorite is my supernatural sleepover. I'm talking about a really spooky event with ghost stories, fortune-telling, and mysterious creaks and bumps in the night! My friends tell me I have a flair for the dramatic, and they even say I sometimes go overboard! But as far as I'm concerned, a spooky sleepover can't have too much drama, so listen closely and I'll tell you what to do to have a super supernatural sleepover of your own.

Invitations

This is what you'll need to make really great spooky invitations that will definitely get your friends into the (gulp) spirit of the night:

- Thick black construction paper
- A silvery metallic pen (You can buy these at almost any stationery store.)
- A pair of good strong scissors for paper

Trace the outline of a ghost, a skeleton, a witch, a cat, or a haunted house. Draw the shape on black construction paper and carefully cut it out. Use the metallic pen to write your invitation. It should read something like this:

Come to a spooky sleepover . . . if you dare.
An eerie night of thrills, chills, and mystery
awaits!
The haunting will begin on (date)
at (time)   at (address)
Bring your sleeping bag,
but please leave your
black cat at home!
RSVP (phone number)

You can trace the invitation on page 83, or you can write your own. Use your imagination. Remember, the spookier the better!

Food

Although I can never resist treats like Kate's super-fudge, I do *try* to watch what I eat. But for some reason all this spooky stuff really scares up my appetite. Here's one of my favorite snacks — vegetable sticks:

Cut the following vegetables into thin strips: carrots, green and red peppers, broccoli, celery.

These vegetable sticks are lo-cal and can look very sophisticated if you take the time to arrange them just right on a big round platter. I often add flowers made out of radishes to mine for an extra touch of red.

For the main meal, here's another of my favorite recipes: tacos. These tacos not only taste great, they look great because they're red and white — two of my favorite colors. If only I could figure out a way to make them red, white, and black! (We told her burning the meat was going a little too far! *Lauren, Kate,* and *Patti*)

Stephanie's Red-and-White Tacos

1 lb ground beef
12 taco shells
lettuce, chopped (optional)
tomato, diced
white cheddar cheese, grated
onions, diced
chili powder
cayenne pepper

Cook the ground beef and onions (if you like onions) in a large skillet until the meat is brown. Carefully drain the grease. If you like spicy food, add a tablespoon of chili pepper to the meat. If you like really spicy food — like I do — add just a tiny bit of cayenne. (Half a pinch: cayenne is super spicy!) Place the shells on a plate. Then put the tomato, cheese, onions, and lettuce in bowls, and turn your guests loose. The lettuce is optional because green is *not* one of my favorite colors. Makes 12 tacos.

When the ghost stories start, I always like to have plenty of comforting snacks to munch on. My mom has made her yummy peanut-butter-chocolate-chip cookies for as long as I can remember. No matter how spooked I am, they always make me feel safe! For a fun supernatural touch, try making these cookies in the shape of witches, black cats, or grinning jack-o'-lanterns!

Mrs. Green's Peanut-Butter-Chocolate-Chip Cookies

½ cup margarine or butter, left out to get soft
½ cup chunky peanut butter
1 cup sugar
1 cup firmly packed brown sugar
1 egg
½ teaspoon vanilla extract
1¼ cup all purpose flour
¾ teaspoon baking soda
½ teaspoon baking powder
½ teaspoon salt
1 cup semisweet chocolate chips (I like mini
    chips even better. *Kate*)

In a large mixing bowl, cream the butter or margarine. Add the peanut butter, sugar, brown sugar, egg, and vanilla. (If you have an electric mixer this will be much easier! *Patti*) In another bowl, mix together the flour, baking soda, baking powder, and salt. Slowly add the dry ingredients to the wet ones until everything is mixed together. Add the chocolate chips and mix them in with a spoon. Wash your hands. Then split the dough in two, and on a clean surface, roll each half with clean hands until it is a tube 1½ inches in diameter. (It will look like a peanut-butter-chocolate-chip snake! *Lauren*) Wrap in waxed paper and chill in the refrigerator for at least three hours. Unwrap and cut into slices ¼ inch thick. Place on a slightly greased cookie sheet. Bake for 8 to 10 minutes in a 350 degree oven. Makes about 5 dozen medium-sized cookies.

When I was eight my parents sent me to summer camp. I quickly discovered that I hate camping, campfire songs, and unlike Patti, I hate nature hikes. Camp could have been totally awful, but fortunately I discovered two things I still really like: s'mores and ghost stories.

Supernaturally Super S'mores

I call these indoor s'mores because you don't need a campfire to make them. (They're called s'mores because they are so good, you'll want some more. *Lauren*)

1 box graham crackers (you'll have some left over)
1 chocolate bar for each guest
1 bag marshmallows

Preheat the oven to 300 degrees. Arrange the graham crackers on a cookie sheet; top with a piece of chocolate, somewhat smaller than the cracker, and two or three marshmallows. Put them in the oven and watch them carefully! They are done when the marshmallows are soft and warm.

Games and Activities

• *Haunted House.* Before the party begins, transform your room into a chamber in a haunted mansion, with plenty of dark corners, cobwebs, and ghostly footsteps! Dangle all sorts of slimy, creepy crawly creatures from the ceiling! Rubber snakes, spiders, and bats work really well. (You can buy them at many toy stores and any shop that specializes in magic.) Next, put a red light bulb in your lamp — it'll give your room a really ghoulish glow! Then put up big black cut-outs of witches, skeletons, and black cats on the walls and windows.

On the night of the sleepover, lead your friends on a tour through your haunted chamber. Blindfold them. Then make them put their hands inside a mystery box and guess what's inside. Use objects like peeled grapes, which feel like eyeballs, or spaghetti, which feels like brains. Jell-O and prepackaged slime also work really well! I know. Even Kate, who's usually pretty levelheaded, screamed when she put her hand in Jell-O. And when we tried it on Lauren, we couldn't calm her down for a whole week!

• *Myra the Magician*. You be the magician. (This is especially fun if you like to perform as much as Stephanie does. *Lauren*) Go to the library and read up on tricks you can perform. You might also check out a hobby store for some simple, inexpensive equipment. Disappearing ink, rope tricks, and the old coin trick are some of my favorites. Here's how Magician Myra's Disappearing Coin Trick works:

You'll need a dime, a handkerchief, a paper cup, and scissors.

Cut a slot into the cup about ⅛ inch from the bottom. The hole should be big enough for a dime to fit through, and no bigger. To perform the trick, drop the dime into a paper cup, and cover the cup with a handkerchief. Shake the cup so that everyone can hear the coin rattle. Shaking the cup will shake the dime into your hand, but nobody will be able to see it! Shout a magic word, like "Abracadabra!" While you whisk the handkerchief away from the cup, slip the dime into your pocket. Show your friends the empty cup, and then slowly take the dime from your pocket.

Here's a tip from one who knows: It pays to practice ahead of time.

You will be such a hit with the coin trick that your guests will demand an encore. Try this one:

• *Wanda Witch's Bedeviling Card Trick.* This trick really isn't hard — after all, *I* learned it. Here's how it works. Put on a black skirt and wrap yourself in a black scarf to become Wanda Witch, gifted with amazing magical abilities and able to read people's minds! Fan out a deck of cards in front of you, and have a friend pick a card from the deck. Take the card without looking at it. Hold it up to show the rest of the group. Here's the tricky part. Hold the card with the back facing you, so everyone thinks you can't see it. Then quickly fold the bottom corner back until you can see the number and suit of the card.

It's not hard, but it *does* take time to get it just right. It took me a whole week. Once you've seen the card, the rest is simple. Just put the card back in the deck. Then go into your Wanda Witch act, which should say something like this: "I think I see something red. Ahhh . . . I think it's a diamond . . . no, a heart . . . five hearts. The card is . . . the five of hearts!"

I guarantee, your friends will be amazed! (I guarantee — we were amazed at what a ham Stephanie can be! *Kate*)

• *Palm Reading*. Lots of people believe your palms provide clues about the kind of person you really are. I don't know about that, but it can be fun to see whether what your palm says about you matches what you think about yourself. People have read palms for thousands of years. When I read mine, I found out that I am impulsive, creative, and assertive! (Surprise! *Lauren*) Here are a few basics to get you started:

Life Line: Your life line tells you a great deal about your personality. A long life line means you are a very active person with a great deal of energy. You like to be out doing things all the time. A short life line means you prefer staying at home and prefer mental to physical activities. If your life and head lines start at the same place, it means you are very well-balanced and may even be shy and cautious. If, however, they begin from different places, you are probably stubborn and impulsive like me.

Head Line: If your head line follows a straight line across your hand then you are probably quite a practical person. If it slopes down, you probably are quite sensitive and tend to have an overactive imagination! (That explains it! Lauren's looks like a ski jump! *Kate*)

Love or Heart Line: If your heart line is straight it means that you are a head-in-the-clouds type. You idolize people and can sometimes be disappointed. You always think the best of people — especially people you are close to. If the heart line curves you tend to be more down-to-earth.

Fate Line: If you have a strong fate line you tend to be someone who is determined to have your own way — no matter what! A wavy fate line means you have a hard time standing up for yourself and must learn to be more outspoken. (Lauren, are you listening? *Kate*)

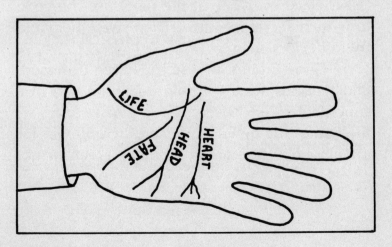

• *Secret Codes.* Nothing is more fun than a secret code. Here's one of my favorites. It's perfect for a supernatural sleepover because any word spelled with it sounds just like something a witch would mumble over a bubbling cauldron!

A = Z	G = T	M = N	S = H	Y = B
B = Y	H = S	N = M	T = G	Z = A
C = X	I = R	O = L	U = F	
D = W	J = Q	P = K	V = E	
E = V	K = P	Q = J	W = D	
F = U	L = O	R = I	X = C	

Here's how my name sounds: Hgvkszmrv Tivvm. Better than plain old Stephanie Green, right? Have everyone at the party use the code to write a secret message. Then swap them and try to decipher them!

• *Ghost Stories.* In case you haven't guessed, ghost stories are my absolute favorite part of a supernatural sleepover. I *love* ghost stories — the scarier the better! (See *Kate's Camp-Out* for a really good one about a creepy green hand.)

With this ghost story game you're bound to hear some real chillers.

Here's how to play. Before you start, get a long piece of twine or clothesline — about two feet of rope for every guest at your party. Tie a knot a third of the way down the rope. Then tie up the ends so that it forms a big circle — big enough so that everyone in your group can hold onto it. (The rope should now have two knots in it.) Now, the fun can begin. Get everyone to sit in a circle and take hold of the rope. To get things rolling, start telling a ghost story. While you tell it, pull the rope through your hands. When you feel a knot, stop immediately. The person who is closest to or touching the other knot must now pick up the story where you left off. We usually play until someone comes up with a really spooky ending, or we all burst out laughing, depending on which comes first. (Guess which one usually does! *Kate*) A final word of warning: Some of the scariest ghost stories I've ever heard — and I'm pretty much an expert by now — have been made up by people playing this game!

Final Tips

Halloween is one of the best times to have a scary sleepover. If you do have your supernatural sleepover on Halloween, you can make orange and black your theme colors and get your friends to come in costume. However, Halloween isn't the only time to have a spooky sleepover. If you're anything like me, any time of year is good for some scary fun and a wild costume. So, have a great time and let me know if you come up with any great new supernatural sleepover ideas!

Chapter 4
Kate's Movie Madness Sleepover

I'm Kate Beekman. As my Sleepover Friends can tell you, I'm crazy about movies: horror movies, romances, foreign films, and especially the old-fashioned black-and-white kind. One day I plan to direct movies of my own, which you'll be able to see at a theater near you! Until then, I'll have to be happy making home movies with the Sleepover Friends' video camera and watching as many as I can. If you'd like to have your own movie madness sleepover (sure to be an Academy-Award-winning event), this is the chapter for you.

Invitations

Here's what you'll need for the invitations:

- Construction paper in bright, attention-getting colors (Some of my favorites are royal blue, magenta, and lemon yellow.)
- A glitter pen (You can buy these at most stationery or drug stores.)
- Stick-on glitter stars and moons (Again, you can find these at many stationery and art supply stores.)
- A magazine with pictures of your favorite TV and movie stars
- A pair of good paper scissors
- Paper glue (I like to use a glue stick.)

Imagine you're designing your own movie poster or movie marquee. You can trace lots of neat shapes onto your construction paper, including a star, a camera, or a popcorn box. Carefully cut the shapes out and decorate them with glitter stars and moons, or pictures of your favorite stars. (I'd put Kevin DeSpain and Marcy Monroe on mine! *Stephanie*) Then, using the glitter pen, write out the invitation like this:

World Premiere!
You are cordially invited to attend
the gala premiere of
THE SLEEPOVER PARTY

Directed by: (your name)
Opening night: (the date and time)
Screening at: (your address)
Bring your sleeping bag for a night of
   movie madness, mayhem, and munchies!
RSVP (your phone number)

My invitation is on page 85.

Food

What's a great movie without munchies? If you're like me, you probably can't imagine watching your favorite films without popcorn. Make plenty of it, topped with fresh hot butter, salt, or Parmesan cheese.

For dinner I usually serve sandwiches — easy to handle in front of the TV. My Hollywood Tuna Melt is always a hit.

Hollywood Tuna Melt

2 cans white chunk tuna (6½ oz)
6 slices bread, or six bagel halves
6 slices American or cheddar cheese
6 tomato slices
mayonnaise
pepper (optional)
dill weed (optional)

Preheat the oven to 350 degrees.

To make tuna salad: Empty the cans of tuna into a medium size bowl. Add mayonnaise until the tuna holds together. If you like, add a pinch of pepper and a pinch of my special ingredient — dill weed.

Toast the bread or bagels. Spoon the tuna salad onto toast and top with a slice of tomato and a slice of cheese. Place on a cookie sheet, and heat until cheese melts. Makes 6 open-faced sandwiches.

Lauren, the toughest food critic I know, agrees these tuna melts are delicious. And Patti, who knows all about nutrition, says they're good for you, too!

After the movie, everybody will probably be ready for another snack. I always make sure to stock up on movie snacktime classics like chocolate-covered raisins, gummy bears, and malted milk balls for my movie madness parties. I also make my all-time favorite dessert — next to my own special super-fudge, of course — my mother's Four-Star Brownies.

Four-Star Brownies

These brownies are super easy to make, and creative at the same time.

1 package brownie mix (23 oz)
½ cup add-ins: Whatever you like! I've tried chocolate chips, M&Ms, almonds, pecans, walnuts, coconut, ground peppermint candies, and peanut butter — and they were all great!

Prepare the brownies according to the package directions. Before cooking, mix in your special additions. Makes 24 large brownies.

Just in case you decide to go for it, I'll also give you the recipe for my real specialty, my renowned Chocolate Marshmallow Super-fudge:

Kate's Chocolate Marshmallow Super-fudge

2½ cups sugar
¼ cup butter or margarine
1 can evaporated milk (5 oz)
1 jar marshmallow cream (7½ oz)
¾ teaspoon salt
¾ teaspoon vanilla
1 package of semisweet chocolate pieces
   (12 oz)

Put the sugar, butter or margarine, evaporated milk, marshmallow cream, and salt together in a large saucepan. Stir over low heat until blended. Turn heat up to medium, so that the mixture boils slowly. Stir constantly for about five minutes — the mixture will get thicker. To make sure that it is done, drop a tiny amount in a cup of cool water. It will hold together in a loose ball if it is done, and separate if it isn't. (Don't forget to keep stirring while you are experimenting! *Lauren*) Remove from heat. Stir in chocolate and vanilla. Keep stirring until chocolate is melted. Pour quickly into a buttered 9- by 9-inch pan. Smooth to the sides of the pan. Rest your stirring arm and let the fudge cool.

After the fudge has cooled, cut into 1-inch squares. Makes more than six dozen small pieces of candy — enough for even a large party. One taste will make you a lifelong fan!

Games and Activities

Sometimes there are lots of great movies on TV, but you can't count on it. With a video cassette recorder, you can plan your own film festival. If your parents don't have one, see if they'll help you rent one from your neighborhood video store or rental center. If you're feeling creative or ambitious, pick movies that fit into a certain theme. Here are some examples:

A Marx Brothers Marathon
    (My first choice. *Patti*)
Watch 'em and Weep Movies
    (Don't forget the hankies!)
Sci-fi Spectacular
    (One of my favorite categories)
Romance Night
    (This is my number-one fave! *Stephanie*)
Animation Festival
Request Night, with choices from friends

The only thing I like almost as much as

watching a great movie is playing these movie games. I hope you and your friends have as much fun playing them as Lauren, Stephanie, Patti, and I do.

• *Trivia Quiz.* Whenever I suggest we play this game, Lauren, Stephanie, and Patti always run away. I don't understand why . . . unless it's 'cause I always win. (It's true — she does! *Lauren*) Divide your party in two groups. Give each group fifteen minutes to come up with ten questions. Then exchange questions and see which team gets the most correct answers.

• *Charades.* Is there a little bit of the actress in you? Stephanie says there certainly is in her! Divide into teams to write the names of your favorite movies or TV shows on slips of paper. Teams trade off to take turns, one player at a time. When it's your turn, you draw a slip from the names written by the other team. First, hold up your fingers to show how many words long your answer will be. Then for each word, tap your fingers on your arm to show how many syllables the word has and which syllable you're acting out. To indicate a two-syllable word, for example, you would tap with two fingers, then with two again if you wanted to act out the second syllable. Pulling on your ear means the correct word "sounds like" the word you are about to act out. For instance, you might point to your nose for "knows," or your ear for the word "here." Once you have the rules down, let your creativity run wild. For extra hints (and a hilarious start) ask your parents to demonstrate this game.

• *Anagrams*. Jumble up the letters in the names of your favorite stars and have all your friends try to guess who they are. This can be harder than it sounds. For example: NEIVK ANPS-EDI is really KEVIN DESPAIN, of course. Another way to play this game is to write down a name and hold it up in front of a mirror. Then everyone has to try and decipher the mirror image.

• *Trading Places*. This is one of the best movie games of all. It's just like being a detective, which would be my second career choice if I hadn't definitely decided to be a film director. This is how it works: Every girl at the party gets up and acts like someone else, anybody from a movie star to a teacher at school. By asking her only yes-or-no questions, the others try to figure out who she is. You not only get to play detective, but to show off your acting skills, too. You should see Lauren pretending to be Marcy Monroe!

• *Let's Put On a Movie.* Make your own movie! This involves a bit of planning, but for a truly spectacular movie madness party it's worth it. Go to your school librarian for help in picking out a play that has the same number of characters as the number of people at your sleepover. (If you're feeling really ambitious, you can even try your hand at writing a movie yourself. I did once. It was called *Invasion of the Killer Mice.*) At your sleepover, hand out copies of the play and let the "star" in everyone come out. The more dramatic everyone is, the better. As the Sleepover Friends can tell you, sometimes the results can be pretty funny!

P.S. If you have a video camera, ask your parents or older brother or sister to tape your dramatic presentation. The only thing more fun than performing in a movie is watching yourself afterwards.

Chapter 5
Patti's New Look Sleepover

Did you ever look at yourself in the mirror and wonder what it would be like if you looked totally different? I did. In fact, I became so convinced I needed a completely new look that I went a little overboard. I put away my regular blue jeans and big navy blue sweater and bought myself a really wild new outfit — a hot pink-and-yellow polka-dotted sweater and a lime-green miniskirt.

Lauren, Kate, and Stephanie thought I'd flipped. (She's not kidding! *Lauren*) And after a while, I decided the real me wasn't happy in a mini. But I *did* have fun trying out a new look, and you will, too. You might even learn something — like what styles you look best in and what you really feel at home in. So get together with some friends, put away your everyday clothes, and explore your hidden personalities for a night!

Invitations

What's a new look party without a new look invitation? Here's what you'll need to make yours:

- Construction paper in the hottest fashion colors
- Good, strong scissors
- Paper glue
- Some of your favorite fashion magazines
- Bright-colored Magic Markers — purple, hot pink, etc.

You can trace and cut out a number of shapes, such as a city skyline or a high top hat. Pick your favorites. Then glue on a contrasting color of construction paper in the same shape. Some of my favorite color combinations are hot pink and lime green (like my outfit!), gray and dusty rose, and purple and yellow. (Red, white, and black? *Stephanie*) For an added touch, glue pictures of your favorite models or the neatest new accessories onto your invitations. (You'll find my invitation on page 87.) Then, in a bright contrasting color, write something like this:

Come as you are to (your name's)
Super Makeover Party
After a night of new fashions,
new hair, and new makeup
you may never be the same!
Location: (your address)
Date: (day and time)
RSVP (your phone number)

Food

At our sleepover parties, I usually leave the food to Lauren, who loves to eat (Is this going to be my only claim to fame? *Lauren*) or Stephanie, who's a creative cook. (What's that supposed to mean? *Stephanie*) I don't really like to cook — something I inherited from my parents. But I do pretty well with this simple recipe for my special dip, which I learned how to make while I was up in Alaska with my family.

Patti's Alaska Dip

1 can chunk, white tuna (7 oz)
1 package creamed cheese (8 oz), left out to
  get soft
½ cup mayonnaise
2 teaspoons lemon juice
1 scallion
1 teaspoon chili sauce

Make sure that you leave the cream cheese out of the refrigerator for about an hour before you start. Drain all the water or oil from the tuna. Clean the scallion and cut into four or five pieces. Put all the ingredients into a food processor or a blender. Blend until well mixed together.

I like to serve the dip with vegetables, nacho chips, or plain old potato chips.

For my main meal I like to serve spaghetti. It doesn't stretch my cooking skills — all you really need to do is boil water! And with this simple sauce Lauren taught me how to make, it's also unbeatably delicious.

Super Sicilian Sauce

The only trick to making great spaghetti sauce is to start two or three hours before you want to eat, because sauce gets better as you cook it.

1½ pounds lean ground beef
¼ cup oil (olive oil is the best, but salad oil is
  good, too)
1 clove garlic, chopped, or ¼ teaspoon garlic
  powder
1 can tomato paste (6 oz)
3 cups tomato juice
salt and pepper to taste
1½ cups water
1 teaspoon sugar
1 teaspoon oregano
1 pound spaghetti for every six guests
¾ cup grated Romano or Parmesan cheese

In a big pot, brown the ground beef. When the meat is brown, carefully drain off any grease into an old jar or can. Add the garlic, tomato paste, tomato juice, water, salt and pepper, sugar, oregano, and oil. Mix everything together and bring to a boil. Turn down the heat and let simmer for at least an hour. Add more water by the tablespoon if the sauce cooks down too much.

Prepare the spaghetti according to the instructions on the package. Drain in a colander, rinse with hot water, shake dry.

Put the spaghetti in one big bowl, the sauce in another, and the cheese in a third. You know what to do from there: Eat!

Dessert is very popular with the Sleepover Friends. Lauren once asked me if I thought life was possible without chocolate! (Is it? *Lauren*) But the last time I tried to bake chocolate chip cookies, my Dad suggested I send the results to NASA to use as rocket fuel! Fortunately, these ice-cream floats are simple, delicious, and pretty, too.

Ice-Cream Floats

Your favorite kind of ice cream for floats
Your favorite kind of soda for floats
Whipped Cream (optional — see recipe on
    page 20)
Straws (optional)
Long spoons (optional)

I like floats with vanilla ice cream and root beer, but Kate likes hers with double chocolate chip ice cream and Dr Pepper. The best thing for a party is to get a variety of flavors of ice cream and kinds of soda. Let your guests pick their favorite flavors and make their own special floats.

What's the whipped cream for? It makes the floats "fluffier." Here's how to do it: Put a teaspoon of whipped cream in the bottom of a tall glass. Then add a scoop or two of ice cream and fill the glass with soda.

Make these floats even prettier by serving them with different colored straws, like electric blue and lime green!

Activities

• *Hair.* A new hairstyle can really change your appearance. Did you ever wonder how you'd look with pink spiked hair? Or whether slicked back hair with rainbow stripes is the look for you? To find out, buy washable mousse or hair gel (available at any drug store) in the wildest colors you can find. (See if you can find some with glitter. *Stephanie*) One word of caution: Make sure there's plenty of water around to clean up afterward. Once at Stephanie's we all put on this really thick purple gel only to discover that the water main to her house had broken, and there was no way to wash off the gel! But don't worry too much. The best thing about mousses and gels is that they don't last forever. So if you find flaming red hair isn't for you, you can always wash it out again! (Stephanie, remember this! *Kate*)

• *Makeup Magic*. All our mothers agree that we're too young for makeup. I wouldn't want to go to all that bother every day, anyway. But it can be fun to experiment — especially on your friends. Try bold shades for a dramatic look or pastels for a more romantic image. One night Stephanie put purple eyeliner on my eyes. She said it transformed me into someone who was mysterious and glamorous. I thought it made me look like a raccoon. (It *was* exotic! *Stephanie*) If your mom has samples from department store giveaways, she might let you have those. Otherwise we like the hypo-allergenic kind from the pharmacy (it doesn't cause allergic reactions). Just be careful not to share eye or lip applicators with anyone else, and be sure to wash your face thoroughly before bedtime unless you want a permanent new look in the morning. (She means zits! *Kate*) (Ugh! *Stephanie*) Have fun finding the perfect look for you! I'm still trying. Actually, the peach lip gloss I bought at Just Juniors looks pretty good.

• *Manicuremania*. I don't wear nail polish very often, but when I do it's usually in a soft pink. Stephanie says that's too tame. She always wears bright red. Sometimes she even wears black! My New Look Sleepover is the time to try out everything. Get wild colors like lemon yellow and sea green. But don't stop there — try painting custom patterns like stripes, stars, moons, polka dots, or even your initials. (Or someone else's. *Stephanie*) Have fun!!!

• *Facials.* After a tough week of school, the Quarks Club, chores, and dealing with a six-year-old brother, I sometimes think I deserve to indulge myself. A facial really does the trick. Stephanie gave me these recipes for facials you can make at home from one of our favorite magazines, *Star Turns*. She swears they really make your skin smoother and clearer. I don't know about that, but they sure make you feel great! (They make me feel like Bullwinkle's breakfast! *Kate*)

All-Over Avocado Face Mask

1 avocado
1 cup of heavy cream or half and half
1 egg

Mix everything together in a blender. Stephanie promises that this stuff will give you a "taut and glowing complexion." You're supposed to leave it on until it dries. Unfortunately, when we tried it, Lauren's dog, Bullwinkle, licked most of it off our faces before it dried, so we really don't know if it works. Let us know!

If you can't get ahold of an avocado, try this instead:

Outrageous Oatmeal Face Mask

2 cups cold, cooked oatmeal
½ cup honey
EITHER ½ cup cream or half and half
OR ¼ cup lemon juice

Stephanie says that you are supposed to use the cream if your skin is dry (like in the winter) and the lemon juice if your skin is oily (like when it is really hot during the summer). I say use whatever you have in the kitchen.

Mix together the oatmeal, honey, and either the cream or lemon juice. Put it on your face, and leave it on for about twenty minutes. Rinse well. (Or you may wake up to find your kitten licking your face — especially if you picked cream! *Kate*)

• *Color Quiz.* The colors you wear can really make a difference in how you look. For example, with the red highlights in my hair and my blue eyes, I look best in colors like navy blue and rust. Colors like yellow — and, unfortunately, hot pink and lime green — don't do much for me at all.

A color quiz is a great way to find out what colors are right for you. You may find out that your best colors are the ones you've preferred all along, but then again, you may be surprised. (Just imagine what Stephanie would do if she found out that red, black, and white are the wrong colors for her! *Kate*) Either way it's a great way to try a new look. Maybe you'll discover your best color is one you never even heard of — like aubergine! (She means eggplant. *Lauren*)

Color Quiz

1. To begin, place your hand on a piece of pure white paper. Does your skin look:
     a. more yellow?
     b. more blue? (It is much easier to decide if you compare with your friends' hands. *Kate*)
     If you choose a, go to question 2 (Patti's skin looks yellow, and Kate's looks golden—which is a more yellow than blue color—*Stephanie*)
     If you answered b, go to question 3.

2. Think about the clothes that you already wear. Do you think you tend to look better in:
     a. browns and greens
     b. pinks and purples (I said b because I look best in my pink jumper, and Patti said a, of course! *Kate*)
   If you chose 2a:
     • Your best colors are "earth colors," like all browns and greens, turquoise, orange, and gold.
     • Stay away from gray, black, pink, and purple.

If you answered 2b:
- Your best colors are all blues, gray, peach, orange, and purple.
- Stay away from black and burgundy.

3. If your skin is blue (Stephanie's olive skin is the bluest, but my skin, which is very pink, looks blue next to Patti's. *Lauren*) ask yourself if you look better in:

a. black and red (a! *Stephanie*)

b. baby blue and light pink (Lauren, this is definitely you. You look fabulous in your light blue-and-pink sweater! *Stephanie*)

If you answered 3a:
- Your best colors are pure white, gray, black, navy, all blues, green, pink, red, bright yellow, or purple.
- You should stay away from brown, tan, orange, and gold.

If you answered 3b:
- Your best colors are brown, blue-gray, all blues, light pink, raspberry, burgundy, maroon, lemon yellow, purple.
- Stay away from black, orange, gold.

• *Face Painting*. This is one way to get a really new look fast. Buy different color tubes of zinc oxide (Yucky name. It's the stuff you put on your face to keep it from getting sunburned. *Stephanie*), or use wild-colored eye pencils or (if you can find it at your local pharmacy), theatrical face paint. Then let yourself go crazy! Paint blue stars on your cheeks or multicolored rainbows around your eyes. Add some glitter and transform yourself into a new you no one will forget in a hurry!

• *Tie Dyeing*. Ever since Stephanie taught the Sleepover Friends how to tie dye, it's been one of our favorite ways to give our clothes a new look. With a little skill (and a little luck), you can turn a plain old boring white T-shirt into a truly fabulous creation. Anything made of white cotton can be tie-dyed: socks, handkerchiefs, jeans, dresses. But before you start, ask your parents' permission. Tie dying can be very messy. (I once learned this the hard way. *Lauren*) Get everything ready ahead of time so that nothing in your house will be accidentally stained or damaged by the dye. These dyes won't come out in the wash. (Good for your creations — bad for everything else. *Kate*) Here's what you'll need to end your new look sleepover in an explosion of color:

- Fabric dye in a variety of bright colors (You can buy basic dyes at any drugstore.)
- White cotton T-shirts (Have your guests bring these.)
- Rubber bands in assorted sizes
- A bucket for each color of dye (Make sure your parents don't mind the buckets being stained.)

Follow the instructions on the packet of fabric dye to get your dyes ready. Before dipping the clothes in the dye, tie rubber bands as tightly as you can where you want designs to appear. Dye won't reach banded parts of the fabric. By using different size rubber bands and dipping the piece of clothing you are dying in a variety of colors, you can create all sorts of neat effects.

Chapter 6
Lauren's All-American Workout

If you've read any of my stories, you know that I love sports and games. The other Sleepover Friends are always teasing me because I go jogging with my older brother, Roger. (Actually, I think I get a lot more exercise giving Roger's dog, Bullwinkle, his daily walk!) When it came time for me to come up with my special sleepover, I decided to center it around my favorite sports activities. The idea isn't to compete, but to have a good time. So on your toes, it's time for Lauren's All-American Workout!

Invitations

You'll definitely want everyone to be on the ball for this sleepover! Get them in the right mood with invitations in the shape of a football, a basketball, a baseball, or a soccer ball. (Check out my invitation on page 89.) As for the colors, the answer is obvious: all-American red, white, and blue! You could word your invitation something like this:

Lace Up Your Sneakers,
Put On Your Sweatsuit
Come on over to (your name)'s
All-American Activities Sleepover!
A fun-filled night of healthy
competition and excitement.
Kickoff begins (date) at (time)
at (address).
RSVP (phone number)

Food

As anyone can tell you, I love to eat! (It's true, she does! *Kate*) Sometimes it seems like almost everything makes me hungry — from boring movies to rainy days. But nothing makes me as hungry as exercise.

With all the activities in my workout sleepover, I'm sure you and your friends will stir up good appetites. Make sure there's plenty of food for everyone. But keep it simple. Start with a bowl of my special dip. (If you've read any of her books, I'm sure you've heard of it! *Kate*) I've been making this dip for years, and I'm not tired of it yet. I bet you will love it, too. (The name of this yummy dip says it all!)

Lauren's Onion Soup-Olives-Bacon-Bits-and-Sour-Cream Dip

1 envelope onion soup mix
1 small can pitted black olives
⅛ cup prepared bacon bits OR
3 strips bacon, fried crisp
2 cups sour cream

To prepare bacon: If you are using bacon strips, fry them in a skillet over a medium heat until they are crisp. Turn off the heat, remove the strips, and drain on a paper towel. Crumble the cooked bacon.

Slice 10 to 12 olives into small pieces.

Mix everything together, and try not to eat it all before your guests arrive! The Sleepover Friends like this dip best with barbecue potato chips, but also try corn chips or chopped veggies.

Follow up the chips 'n' dip with another one of my favorites: all-American hamburgers. They're delicious and good for you, too — especially if you serve them with some fresh tomato and lettuce. My brother, Roger, calls hamburgers "energy food." He should know. Hamburgers are about the only thing he eats! Here's his recipe for Roger's Winning Circle Hamburgers — the burgers that can't be beat!

Roger's Winning Circle Hamburgers

1 lb. ground beef
6 hamburger rolls
1 egg (optional)
1 package onion soup mix (optional)
salt and pepper
Toppings: lettuce, ketchup, mustard,
   mayonnaise, pickles or relish, onions,
   tomatoes, cheese, spaghetti sauce, etc.

Preheat the broiler.

Prepare toppings: slice tomatoes and onions, grate the cheese, heat up spaghetti sauce, etc.

Put the meat in a mixing bowl. If you like, add an egg and a package of onion soup mix to the meat (the egg makes your hamburgers hold together better and the soup is for seasoning). Mix everything together with your hands — wash them first. (This is gross, but it really is the best way.) Form into five or six patties. Put the patties on a foil-covered broiler pan or cookie sheet.

Broil for five minutes, flip and broil on the other side for five minutes. To make sure that they are cooked enough, slice one open a little.

Put the hamburgers on the buns and place

on a plate. Let your guests serve themselves the toppings that they like best.

What's a meal without dessert? My all-American sleepover ends with two all-American classics (that's what my Dad calls them): banana smoothies and apple crisp.

Banana Smoothies

1 banana
1 cup milk
EITHER 1 cup yogurt
OR 1 scoop frozen yogurt
OR 1 scoop vanilla or chocolate ice cream
1 tablespoon honey (optional)

Put everything in a blender and mix. This is an especially healthful recipe if you use yogurt. With ice cream, it is almost like a banana milk shake.

Apple Crisp

2 or 3 red or green apples (depending on their
  size)
¼ cup water
1 teaspoon cinnamon
½ teaspoon salt
1 cup sugar
¾ cup flour
⅓ cup butter, softened

Preheat the oven to 350 degrees.

Peel the apples (if you want) then slice them
and cut away the seeds. Spread four cups of
apples into an 8 × 8 or 9 × 9 baking dish. (You
don't need to have exactly four cups.) Sprinkle
the apples with the water, cinnamon, and salt.

Put sugar, flour, and butter in a mixing bowl
and mix until crumbly. Spread mixture over the
apples. Bake for about 40 minutes.

Games and Activities

• *Organized Events.* What could be more fun — or more American — than a night at the bowling alley? If there's a bowling alley near you, why not arrange to go there with your friends? I've never rolled a strike, but I live in hope. A bowling alley is a surefire winner for a workout sleepover. Other great outings include going ice skating or roller skating or playing miniature golf. Check out what's available in your neighborhood.

• *Backyard Carnival.* If you don't want to go out with your friends, organize a carnival of events in your own backyard. Make booths for Olympic-level competitions such as the bean bag throw or the ever-popular ring toss. Run races like the egg-in-the-spoon race or the three-legged race. One of my favorites is the suitcase-relay race.

Here's how it works. Get an old suitcase and fill it with the funniest old clothes you can find. I put in a hat of my mother's, Dad's old sports jacket, a big apron my mother used to wear, and a pair of my Dad's fishing boots. Put on all the clothes. Then run the race course carrying the suitcase. When you get to the finishing line, take off all the clothes and put them back in the suitcase. (In case you're wondering, nobody manages to run very fast. *Patti*) Then pass the suitcase to the next person who does the same. We played this on my last birthday, and I laughed so hard at how funny everyone looked in my father's boots that I could hardly run. Kate said that was why we lost.

Red, white, and blue ribbons make nice prizes for the winners.

• *Scavenger Hunt.* If you live in a small neighborhood and are friendly with the other people on your street, a scavenger hunt can be a great adventure. The party splits up into teams that go door-to-door looking for items on a list you've handed out. The items should range from ordinary to kooky. (Remember, the nice thing about a scavenger hunt is that the host can play, too.)

First check with the neighbors to make sure they don't mind having you and your friends come knocking on their doors. Then make a list of items for the teams to look for. Include some easy-to-find items and some that will be harder to track down. A good list will have about twenty items. Give a copy of the list to each team. Set a time limit on the search (forty-five minutes to an hour), then turn everyone loose. The first team to return with all the items, or the team to find the most items if no one finds them all, is the winner. Don't forget to take along a bag! Here's our favorite scavenger hunt list:

an oak leaf	a gray pebble
a page from last week's newspaper	a curler
	a yellow sock
a doggy treat	a picture of a fish
a first-prize blue ribbon	a piece of chalk
	fishnet tights
a lollipop	Pete Stone's
an empty ice-cream cone	signature
	a brown shoelace
a catcher's mitt	a foreign coin
sheet music for a piano	a ball of yarn
	a golf ball
a hard-boiled egg	

Looks easy, right? Wait until you start hunting!

• *Indoor Activities.* It's always nice to have a bright sunny day for a sleepover, but if it's raining, snowing, or even worse on the night of your sleepover, you can still work up a flurry of fun with these indoor events!

• *String Hunt.* This is a game I never get tired of, even though it can really tie you up in knots!

Each guest follows a separate trail of string or yarn through the house to find a special prize at the end. It's a good way to start the evening and to break the ice. (And get the string out of the way for the rest of the party. *Stephanie*)

Before your guests arrive, wind trails of string around table legs, banisters, corners of furniture, and doorknobs. Make each trail of string as long as you can, and make sure there is one for each girl. If you can, use a different color yarn for each guest at the party. It looks neat, and it's easier to follow. At the end of each string, hang a small prize, like a candy bar, or plastic bracelets, or colored pencils.

Before long, players will be climbing around, under, and over string paths (and one another) to get to the end.

Don't forget to put away anything breakable beforehand, and have a pair of scissors handy for cleaning up. (Or rescuing an unlucky player. *Kate*)

• *Weekend Workout*. Exercise tires you out, but it also makes you feel great — especially a real all-around workout that stretches all your muscles. Get your friends to bring leotards and an exercise mat or something soft to lie on. Music makes exercise twice as fun, so put on your favorite tape (We always listen to the Boodles. *Stephanie*) and start stretching.

Begin with loosening up exercises like touching your toes or stretching your arms above your head. Then move on to harder exercises like sit-ups, push-ups, and leg stretches. Careful not to overdo it. Sometimes you can stretch your muscles tooooo far! I like to end with a freestyle dance session. Dancing is good exercise because it allows you to use all your muscles at once. It's also fun! Try the latest dance steps, and for a good laugh, get your parents to show you the dances that were popular when they were young. My mom tried to teach us The Bump and I laughed so hard, I almost fell over. But she says moon-walking looks just as funny to her!

Chapter 7
Super Invitations

Invitations are important — they are the first contact with your party that your friends will have. To make them extra special, try these ideas:

Trace the shapes we suggested onto your invitations to make them look unique and to tell your guests what the theme of your party will be. Here are some suggestions on how to use the shapes.

• Make a stencil by tracing the shape onto a piece of thin, plain white typing or note paper. Then trace the shape from your stencil onto your invitation.

• Copy the shape from your stencil onto a

piece of construction paper and cut it out. Either glue the shape onto another piece of paper folded in half or write the sleepover information right onto the shape. Check Chapter 1 for a list of items any sleepover invitation should include, and Chapters 3 through 6 for suggestions of ways to word your invitation.

Special Effects

If you are feeling really creative, try out these extra special invitation effects:

• Combine several of the shapes for a layered effect. For example, a white ghost pasted on top of a black haunted house. Let your imagination run wild!

• With a copying machine, you can make really great invitations! Try enlarging the shapes for big invitations. Or reduce them so that you can fit lots of shapes on one invitation and create a collage effect. Of course, you can also use the machine to copy a finished invitation, so that you don't have to make each one separately.

• Use some invitation accessories! Metallic pens are our favorite because they look great, and they don't make a mess. Calligraphy pens are neat, too! Other things to try: Glitter (best on the border), crepe paper, stickers, ribbons, felt, velvet, buttons, and shells.

I hope that you like the sleepovers Stephanie, Kate, Patti, and I suggested. Speaking from experience, all of them are great fun!

COME TO A SPOOKY SLEEPOVER
IF YOU DARE

AN EERIE NIGHT OF THRILLS, CHILLS, AND MYSTERY AWAITS!

THE HAUNTING
WILL BEGIN

_____
(Date)

AT _____
(Time)

AT MY HOUSE

_____
_____
(Address)

BRING YOUR SLEEPING BAG, BUT PLEASE
LEAVE YOUR BLACK CAT AT HOME!

RSVP _____
(Number)

WORLD PREMIERE!

YOU ARE CORDIALLY INVITED TO ATTEND THE GALA PREMIERE OF

The Sleepover Party

DIRECTED BY:_____
(Name)

OPENING NIGHT:_____
(Date)

SCREENING AT:_____
(Time)

BRING YOUR SLEEPING BAG FOR A NIGHT OF MOVIE MADNESS, MAYHEM, AND MUNCHIES!

RSVP_____
(Number)

Come as
you are to

_____
(Name)

SUPER MAKEOVER PARTY

After a night of new fashions, new hair, and new makeup you may never be the same.

LOCATION _____

_____
(Address)

DATE _____
TIME _____
RSVP _____
(Phone)

LACE
UP YOUR
SNEAKERS
PUT ON YOUR
SWEATSUIT
COME OVER TO _____
(Name)
★ ALL AMERICAN ★
ACTIVITIES SLEEPOVER
A FUNFILLED NIGHT OF
HEALTHY COMPETITION
★ AND EXCITEMENT ★
KICK OFF BEGINS _____
(Date)
AT _____ AT
(Time)
_____
_____
(Address)
RSVP _____
(Number)

Frère Jacques

Méthode de lecture destinée
à l'enseignement de la langue française
aux enfants non francophones
des classes primaires.

Elle comprend :
- le tableau de feutre
- une collection de figurines
- une collection d'étiquettes géantes
(mots et phrases clés des leçons de lecture)
- deux livrets de lecture destinés aux élèves :
— un 1er livret (leçons 1 à 30)
correspondant au 1er livre de langage
— un 2e livret (leçons 31 à 60)
correspondant au 2e livre de langage
- deux cahiers d'exercices écrits :
— un 1er cahier
correspondant au 1er livret de lecture
— un 2e cahier
correspondant au 2e livret de lecture

frère jacques

leçons de lecture

1

J. BERTRAND

J.-L. FREROT

avec la collaboration de
Mlle G. ROMARY

HACHETTE

avertissement

Chaque leçon se présente en 5 parties :
1 - Étude d'une phrase clé : présentation - décomposition - écriture.
2 - Lecture de syllabes (« prononçons »).
3 - Lecture de légendes et de phrases (« comprenons »).
4 - Lecture par phrase d'un court récit (« lecture expressive »).
5 - Lecture courante.

Une phrase clé figure en tête de chaque leçon. Elle est reproduite par les étiqu
mobiles. Elle présente plusieurs mots clés qui contiennent l'élément nouveau étu
Prenons comme exemple la phrase clé de la leçon 26 : *papa arrive avec sa va*
Les trois mots clés : *arrive, avec, valise,* contiennent la lettre *v.*
— La « décomposition » de cette phrase doit permettre de présenter le *v.*
Mais il faut auparavant expliquer la phrase, qui contient :
— certains mots dont le sens est inconnu : *arrive - valise.*
— certaines formes à remettre en mémoire : le possessif *sa* - l'emploi de *avec.*
— *L'explication* sera brève. Elle se fera, sous forme orale, en utilisant le tablea
feutre, ses figurines et ses symboles, comme en langage et selon la même techn
(voir F.J. Leçons de langage - préface).
— *La décomposition* conduite à l'aide du tableau de feutre, des étiquettes et d
paire de ciseaux, progressera en deux étapes :
— une première étape aura pour but d'*isoler les mots clés :* diverses substitu
permettront d'en souligner le rôle (verbe - groupe prépositionnel...) de mettre
évidence la *structure* (et non plus le sens) ;
— une deuxième étape permettra d'isoler la *syllabe* dans le mot, et la *lettre* dan
syllabe, selon le procédé classique.
Les deux tableaux suivants présentent dans son détail, l'étude de la phrase clé : e
cation et décomposition.

TABLEAU 1

Explication de la phrase clé.

● *Avant la leçon, composer au tableau de feutre le cadre convenable* (arbre, mais
placer les personnages (la famille de M. Michaud près de la maison, M. Mich
qui arrive), la situation ainsi évoquée va faciliter la compréhension.

● *Procéder à l'explication,* à l'aide de questions renforcées par le maniement
figurines et *symboles.*

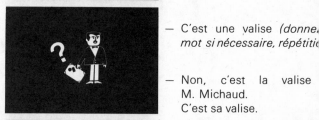

Professeur	Élèves
— Qui est-ce ?	— C'est Mme Michaud.
	— C'est Jean, c'est Moni
— Qui est-ce ?	— C'est M. Michaud, le p
	de Jean et de Monique.
— Qu'est-ce que c'est ?	— C'est une valise *(donne.*
	mot si nécessaire, répétiti
— C'est la valise de M. Saunier ?	— Non, c'est la valise M. Michaud.
	C'est sa valise.
— Que fait M. Mi-chaud ? Il part... ou il arrive ?	— Il arrive.
— Est-ce que M. Mi-chaud arrive avec sa pipe ? avec son sac ? avec sa radio ?	— Non, il arrive avec sa val

ISBN 2.01.002139.8

© Librairie Hachette, 1968.

Regroupement :
— Que dit Jean ?

papa arrive avec sa valise

— Jean dit : papa arrive avec sa valise.

- *Placer la phrase clé* ainsi obtenue sous les yeux des élèves (étiquettes mobiles).
- *La faire répéter* en veillant à la prononciation du « v » (obtenir la sonorité qui le distingue du « f »).
- La faire copier.
- Si des élèves sont jeunes, ils la reconstituent à l'aide des étiquettes individuelles.

TABLEAU 2

Décomposition de la phrase clé.

papa arrive avec sa valise.

- *De la phrase au mot :*
— *Faire reconnaître* les mots déjà acquis en lecture : *papa - sa.*
— *Isoler* successivement chaque mot nouveau ; exemple :

papa	avec sa valise
arrive	

— *Substituer* à ce verbe inconnu, des verbes déjà appris en lecture, par exemple : *passe - court - tombe.*

papa	passe	avec sa valise
	tombe	
	arrive	

— *Faire lire* chaque phrase ainsi modifiée.
— *Procéder de même* pour « *valise* » en utilisant des mots connus de même valeur grammaticale : *radio, pipe...*
— *Reconstituer,* après chaque substitution, la phrase de départ.
— *Exercices individuels :*
Découpage de la phrase clé (étiquettes individuelles).
Substitution d'étiquettes :
a) avec modèle au tableau sous les yeux
b) sans modèle, en changeant un mot ou deux.
Dictée.

- *Du mot à la lettre :*
Découper les trois mots en *syllabes phonétiques :*

valise	avec	arrive
va	vec	rive

Aligner verticalement les trois syllabes : un élève vient montrer l'élément commun le « v » :

va
vec
rive
v

— *Détacher* le « v », l'écrire au tableau en script et en cursive.
— *Le faire « entendre »* (ici, c'est une consonne sonore, on peut la chanter).
— *Faire trouver* les mots connus où le même son est entendu (chasse aux mots).
— Faire écrire le « v ».

Le nouvel élément, le « v », n'a été identifié que dans quelques syllabes. Il faut él[...]
cette découverte, varier méthodiquement la *structure des syllabes* en partant [...]
syllabes clés :

— Par remplacement de la voyelle voisine : *va... vi... vou...*
— Par adjonction d'un son-consonne : *vi... vide... vite...*
— *Par changement de position* du « v » :

        position médiane : *avec... il va vite... il vous parle...*
        position finale : *rive... arrive... couve...*

D'autre part le « v », consonne *sonore* est souvent prononcé par les non francopho[...]
comme le « f », consonne *sourde*, déjà étudiée : nous opposerons systématiquer[...]
ces deux consonnes dans un exercice spécial qu'on peut enrichir, si nécessaire[...]
tableau noir : *fa... va... fé... vé...*

Nous ne faisons intervenir, dans la composition des syllabes, que les sons déjà con[...]
Nous ne tiendrons pas compte du sens des syllabes ou mots utilisés, le but des e[...]
cices étant seulement de créer, à la vue des signes, les *réflexes articulatoires*. Il fa[...]
donc obtenir une lecture de *plus en plus rapide*, opérer *dans l'ordre*, puis *en désor[...]*
Il faut exiger une prononciation « à la française », (accents-élisions du *e* final (« m[...]
de *couvé, lavé*, etc.).

● *La « maison des syllabes »* : cet accessoire utile surtout pour les enfants de 6 à 8 [...]
peut être utilisé à partir de la leçon 8. Il a la forme d'une *maison* de 30 cm × 40 [...]
Trois glissières découpées dans les fenêtres permettent d'introduire *trois bandes* [...]
tonnées où le maître inscrit progressivement les différents signes alphabétiques con[...]

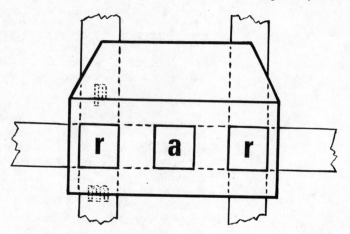

On peut ainsi composer, par simple glissement des bandes, de nombreuses syllab[...]
On pourra fabriquer, pour chaque élève, une maison des syllabes en réduct[...]
(8 cm × 12 cm).

Cet accessoire transforme en jeux les divers exercices portant sur les syllabes [...]
notamment *les dictées de syllabes* avec *contrôle phonétique*.

Compréhension - expression - lecture courante.

● *« Comprenons »* : sous la rubrique « comprenons » on trouvera des images, d[...]
il faut lire la légende, ainsi que de courtes phrases.

Les images illustrent le *vocabulaire nouveau*, ainsi que des *mots déjà étudiés* [...]
langage, qui contiennent la lettre « v ».

L'effort de déchiffrage se complète ici par l'effort de *compréhension*.

● *« Lecture expressive »* : les phrases composent ici un court récit, brassant le vo[...]
bulaire nouvellement acquis, et l'ancien. Le respect du *rythme* et la recherche [...]
l'intonation juste, s'ajoutent au travail de déchiffrage et de compréhension.

● *« Lecture courante »* : le texte de lecture courante (écrit en petits caractères) p[...]
met le réemploi constant des éléments étudiés dans un texte plus riche, plus motiva[...]
mobilisant toutes les acquisitions de la méthode. Ce texte ne peut être abordé qu'[...]
moment des révisions, ou pour les plus jeunes, en fin d'année scolaire.

pa

jean

jacques

aman

monique

simone

net

médor

nicolas

le chat de monique va sous le lit

le chat de monique va sous le lit

mi	net

mi

i

i

mo	nique

nique

i

i

Chasse aux mots connus où l'on entend « **i** » (**ami, joli, ici**...)
— en choisir 3
— écrire ces mots au tableau noir (2 écritures : script, liée)
— faire trouver les « **i** »
— les faire repasser à la craie rouge.

lit   minet   monique   pipe

mi - lit - le lit de mimi

URE EXPRESSIVE

1 <u>voilà</u>* monique.
2 voilà minet.
3 le chat de monique.
4 le lit de monique.
5 voilà le chat de monique.
6 voilà le lit de monique.
7 *le chat va sous le lit.*
8 *minet va sous le lit de monique.*
9 *monique va sous le lit.*

* à présenter globalement.

URE COURANTE

1 Monique est sur son lit. Elle lit un livre.
2 Voilà Mimi. Elle va vite sous le lit.
3 Qui est Mimi ?
4 C'est une jolie petite souris grise.
5 Que fait-elle sous le lit de Monique ?
6 Elle rit, elle rit,
7 Minet, le petit chat de Monique, n'est pas ici.
8 Il est parti samedi pour Paris.
9 Il est parti dans une valise.
10 Il est parti manger toutes les petites souris de Paris.

ÉE

1 Voilà Minet — 2 Mimi, la petite souris — 3 va vite — 4 sous le lit de Monique.

médor a le sac de papa

médor a le sac de papa

a	**sac**	**pa**
a	**a**	**a**
a	*a*	*a*

Chasse aux mots connus (**ami – table...**)
(voir indications pédagogiques à la leçon 2).

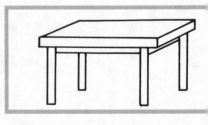

sac   papa   table

1 le sac de monique. 2 monique a le sac.
3 le chat de papa.   4 papa a le chat.

TURE EXPRESSIVE

1 voilà médor.
2 voilà le sac.
3 papa a le sac.
4 simone a le sac de papa.
5 le papa de simone a le sac.
6 jacques, voilà le chat !

7 *jacques a le sac de simone.*
8 *le chat va sous le sac.*
9 *médor va sous le lit.*

TURE COURANTE

1 Mon chapeau ! où est mon chapeau ?
2 Maman, regarde, il n'est pas sur la table ?
3 Jacques, tu n'as pas mon chapeau ?
4 Non, papa.
5 Mon chat ! où est mon chat ?
6 Mina, regarde, il n'est pas dans ton sac ?
7 Jacques, va au jardin, regarde dans la salade !
8 Non, Monique, il n'est pas là.
9 Les voilà ! Sous la table. Le chat est assis dans le chapeau de papa.

ÉE

1 Papa, regarde Mina — 2 Elle est sous la table — 3 avec le chat.

4

maman, où est ma poupée ?

maman, où est ma poupée ?

où est	**poupée**
ou	pou
ou	**ou**
ou	*ou*

Chasse aux mots connus (**rouge - écoute - il joue...**)
(indications pédagogiques à la leçon 2).

poupée   poule   poussin

PRONONÇONS *pou - man - de - la - ma - pée - est*
où est la malade ?

TURE EXPRESSIVE

1 où est la poupée de monique ?
2 la poupée est là.
3 où va la <u>souris</u>* ?
4 la souris va sous le lit.
5 papa, où est la souris ?
6 la souris est sous le lit de simone.
7 maman, où est ma poule ?
8 *où est la poule de monique ?*
9 *ma poule est là, sous le sac de papa.*

TURE COURANTE

1 Jean est dans la cour avec Jacques.
2 Ils jouent au ballon.
3 Monique joue à la poupée.
4 Voilà la petite poule rouge avec ses poussins.
5 « Où vas-tu petite poule rouge ?
6 Pourquoi cours-tu ? »
7 La pauvre poule court partout : derrière le ballon, sur les jouets de Monique, sous le lit de la poupée.
8 « Petits ! petits ! vite, voilà le chat. »
9 La poule a tous ses poussins sous elle.
10 Voilà Minet. Il tourne, tourne devant la poule et... bonjour !

TÉE

1 Où est la poule ? — 2 Elle est sous le lit — 3 avec la souris — 4 Le chat n'est pas là.

Syllabes en opposition

li	la	lou		mi	ma	mou
pi	pa	pou		si	sa	sou

Groupes avec accent tonique

voilà le nid de la souris. voilà le nid de la poule
voilà le lit de la poupée. voilà la poupée de ma

il part pour paris. le loup va sous le lit.
il part pour lima. minou va sous la table

1 papa - simone - la poupée - monique
2 la poule - le sac - le lit - le chat
3 ma - mé - man - pou - pa - pée
4 le - de - dor - est - va - sous
5 a - ou - i - i - a - i - ou - a - a - ou
6 i - ou - i - a - a - ou - i - i - ou - a
7 simone - le sac - la poupée - le chat.
8 le lit - papa - la poule - monique.

1 jean, où est médor ?
2 voilà médor !
3 voilà la souris, là, sous le lit.
4 où va le chat de monique ?
5 minet va sous la table.
6 *voilà la poule de monique.*
7 *la poile a le sac de la poupée.*
8 *maman, où est la poupée ?*
9 *la poupée est sous le sac de papa.*

1 Un petit chat gris, c'est Minet.
2 Une petite souris grise, c'est Mimi.
3 Une petite poule rouge, c'est Gloussette.
4 Un joli petit poussin, c'est Piou.
5 Une jolie petite poupée, c'est Mina.
6 Voilà tous les amis de Monique.
7 Ah ! J'oublie Médor.
8 Où est Médor ?
9 Il est toujours sous la table... sage comme une image.

la poupée est à côté de la télé*

la poupée est à côté de la télé

té lé		poupée		à côt
té lé		pé		té
é é		**é**		**é**
é é		é		é

Chasse aux mots connus

poupée	télé	vélo	cinéma

té -pé-lé-mé-la-de-est-pou-co

PRONONÇONS

COMPRENONS

pépé   mémé

l'épée de jean   le pâté de monique

* Avant de présenter cette phrase, bien mettre en évidence la forme **« est à côté de »** pa
diverses substitutions de figurines et d'étiquettes.

LECTURE EXPRESSIVE

1 minet est à côté de médor.
2 le chat <u>regarde</u>* la souris à la télé.
3 médor regarde papa.
4 le sac de papa est à côté de médor.
5 maman, regarde ma poupée !
6 *la poupée est à côté de monique.*
7 *regarde le lit de ma poupée.*
8 *le lit de la poupée est à côté de la télé.*

LECTURE COURANTE

1 Le dimanche, après déjeuner, papa regarde la télé. Médor est à côté.
2 Maman fait du thé et du café.
3 Un peu de café pour papa, beaucoup de thé pour elle.
4 Moi, je ne bois ni thé ni café, alors, je vais jouer avec mes amis.
5 Je fais du vélo, je joue à la balle ou je vais au cinéma.
6 « Est-ce que tu vas à l'école à vélo ?
7 — Non, c'est le vélo de mon père. Je le prends pour aller chez l'épicier ou pour jouer le dimanche.
8 — Mais tu es un voleur, Jacques ! »

DICTÉE

1 Le chat est un voleur — 2 Il boit le café de Papa — 3 Je vais acheter du café et du thé.

médor mord la robe de monique

médor mord la robe de monique

médor	**mord**	**robe**	**monique**
dor	mor	robe	mo
o	o	o	o
o	*o*	*o*	*o*

Chasse aux mots connus

   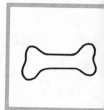

médor · · · · robe · · · · monique · · · · os

dor - ro - mord - mo - mé - la - de

mo - mor - dor - la - mé - de

maman est à côté de la télé.   jacques va au cinéma.

la robe est à côté de médor   monique va à l'école

1 où est la robe de ma poupée ?

2 la robe de la poupée est sous la télé.

3 monique regarde sous la télé.

4 médor mord la robe de la poupée.

5 maman, médor mord ma poupée.

6 la souris va à côté de monique.

7 le chat mord la souris.

8 *médor, minet mord la souris.*

9 *médor mord le chat.*

10 *la souris va à côté de médor.*

1 Le chat dort à côté de Monique.

2 Il a un os sous la patte.

3 Médor vole l'os de Minet et sort vite dans le jardin.

4 « Qu'est-ce que c'est ? dit Minet ; mon os, voleur ! »

5 Monique rit. Elle court derrière son chat.

6 « Médor, ici ! donne l'os à Minet.

7 — Écoute, j'ai du chocolat dans ma poche. Il est pour toi si tu apportes l'os. »

8 Mais Médor n'écoute pas ; il court, court encore.

1 Il donne du chocolat à Monique — 2 Médor dort à côté du chat — 3 Le chat mord la souris — 4 Simone va à l'école.

papa répare la radio

papa répare la radio

ré	pare
r	r
ꭆ	ꭆ

ra
r
ꭆ

PRONONÇONS

ra*	pari	paré	par	par
ri	riri	rira	rir	rir
ro	miri	miro	mor	por
rou	pourri	pourra	pour	pèr
ré	méri	mérou		

COMPRENONS

cours, souris !   dors, médor !   médor mord le rat

la roue   le repas   la souris court <u>derrière</u>* la ra

1 regarde, médor rit.
2 « où est médor ? — là, derrière. »

* Les élèves déchiffrent et lisent les syllabes suivantes sans que la maîtresse explique le se

ECTURE EXPRESSIVE

1   la poupée dort derrière le sac.
2   la souris mord la robe.
3   minet est à côté. regarde, minet.
4   où est la souris ? là, derrière le sac.
5   à côté de minet,
6   sous la robe de la poupée.
7   cours, médor, cours !
8   *médor mord le sac de papa.*
9   *minet mord médor.*
10 *la souris rit .*

LECTURE COURANTE

1   Qui est-ce qui répare la roue du vélo ? C'est papa.
2   Qui est-ce qui prépare le repas ? C'est maman.
3   Et Jean, et Monique, qu'est-ce qu'ils font ?
4   Jean écoute la radio et Monique regarde la télé.
5   Où sont les bêtes ?
6   Minet est derrière l'arbre. Il dort.
7   Médor court dans le jardin, derrière un rat.
8   Une voiture rouge roule dans la rue. Elle s'arrête derrière la porte du jardin.
    C'est Simone et son frère. Bonjour les amis !

9

la poule dort, elle est malade

la poule dort, elle est malade

la	**poule**	**elle**	**malade**
l	l	ll	l
l	*l*	*ll*	*l*

PRONONÇONS

la

lou	lour
li	lir
lo	lor
la	lar

poule

roule	oul
pile	il
pole	ol
pale	al

COMPRENONS

le colis est lourd

il roule sous le lit

monique lit à l'école

voilà le loup, il mord

1 regarde la poupée, elle dort.
2 regarde le chat, il dort.

16

LECTURE EXPRESSIVE

1 jean, regarde le chat à la télé.
2 il va derrière la souris.
3 regarde, il mord la souris.
4 voilà médor, il est sous le lit, il dort.
5 monique regarde la poupée.
6 elle est sur le lit, elle dort.
7 elle est pâle*, elle est malade.
8 où est la robe de la poupée ?
9 regarde, elle est là, derrière la télé.
10 où est la poule ? elle est sous le sac.

LECTURE COURANTE

1 « Silence ! ne parle pas. La poule est malade.
2 — Qu'est-ce qu'elle a ? — Elle a mal à la langue.
3 — Où est-elle ? — Elle est là, sur son nid, elle dort.
4 — Gloussette, ma belle, ouvre le bec : voilà du sel pour ta langue malade. »

1 « Ah, voilà papa. Il apporte un gros colis. C'est lourd !
2 — Qu'est-ce qu'il y a dans le colis ?
3 — Il y a une belle balle, un livre d'école, un petit lit de poupée et un joli lapin en chocolat. »

DICTÉE

1 La poule est malade. — 2 Elle dort. — 3 Monique dort sur le lit. — 4 Médor dort sous le lit.

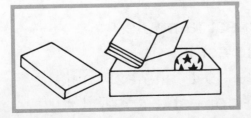

PRONONÇONS

Groupes avec accent tonique

la belle robe	sur le nid ?	elle regarde la télé.
la belle radio	sur le lit ?	il apporte le colis.
la belle roue	sur le livre ?	elle ouvre la porte.
la belle règle	sur le colis ?	il répare la balle.

1 monique - la robe - la radio

2 la télé - la souris - médor

3 médor - la robe - la télé

4 la souris - monique - la radio

5 ma - mé - mo - mord - dor - té

6 la - ta - lou - rou - ré - lé - lou - rou

7 *ris - ri - li - il est - elle est*

8 *ir - il - lir - or - ol - lor*

9 *al - ral - lar - oul - our - lour - roul*

LECTURE EXPRESSIVE

1 où est la poule ?

2 elle est sur le sac.

3 elle dort, elle est malade.

4 médor est à côté, il regarde.

5 le sac roule, il est lourd.
6 médor va sous le sac.
7 il mord la poule.
8 où est le chat ?
9 *il est derrière le lit.*
10 *il regarde la souris.*
11 *la souris dort sous le lit.*

CTURE COURANTE

« Marie, dit le père, je pars pour 3 jours à la ville. Ne sors pas de la maison, n'ouvre pas la porte et ne parle à personne.
Regarde sur la table cette belle boîte rouge. Ne l'ouvre pas ! »
Le père sort, prend son vélo et s'en va...
Qu'est-ce qu'il y a dans cette boîte rouge ?
Marie tourne et retourne la boîte et elle l'ouvre.
Hi ! Ce sont des souris !
Elles courent partout dans la maison : sur le lit, sous la table, derrière la télé, devant la radio.
Une souris mord la robe de Marie. Pauvre Marie !

CTÉE

1 Où est la poule ? — 2 Elle est sur le sac — 3 Elle dort — 4 Elle est malade.

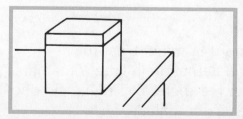
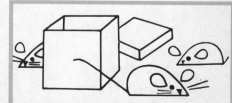

voilà madame michaud,
c'est la maman de monique

voilà madame michaud, c'est la maman de moniqu

ma	dame	**mi**	chaud	**ma**	man	**mo**	nique

m   **m**   **m**   **m**   **m**   **m**

m   m   m   m   m   m

PRONONÇONS

ma	**mi**	**simone**	**dame**
mi	mir	mine	lime
mo	mor	more	rome
ma	mar	malle	lame
mou	mour	moule	
mé		mène	
		mère	

COMPRENONS

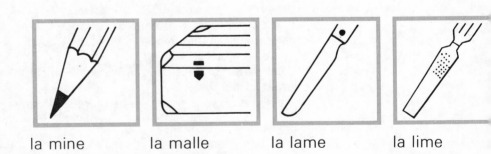

la mine   la malle   la lame   la lime

1 il mord la mine, c'est mal.
2 papa demande la lime à maman.
3 c'est ma mère, elle mène simone à l'école.
4 mémé est malade.

TURE EXPRESSIVE

1 jacques, où est ma poupée ?
2 demande à maman !
3 maman, où est ma poupée ?
4 elle est là, à côté de minet.
5 minet dort à côté de ma poupée.
6 voilà madame la souris.
7 regarde maman, elle mord minet.
8 *miaou ! miaou ! minet a mal.*
9 *voilà la mère de madame michaud.*
10 *c'est la mémé de monique michaud.*

TURE COURANTE

« Bonjour Madame Michaud ! Comment allez-vous ?
— Moi, ça va, merci ! Mais Monique est malade. Elle ne dort pas, elle ne mange pas, elle a mal partout. Ma mère est avec elle à la maison.
— Où allez-vous ce matin ?
— Je vais au marché. Il me faut des pommes de terre, des tomates, un melon et un gigot de mouton pour midi.
— Et votre mari, qu'est-ce qu'il fait ?
— Il répare sa moto. Il la répare tous les jours, mais elle ne marche jamais. »

TÉE

1 Maman, où est la malle ? — 2 Il y a un malade — 3 Demande qui c'est — 4 C'est la mère de Simone.

nicolas donne de la limonade à simone

nicolas donne de la limonade à simone

ni	co	las		donne		li	mo	nade		si	mone

n   **nn**   **n**   **n**

n   *nn*   *n*   *n*

PRONONÇONS

ni			**donne**
no	mono	nor	mone
na	mina	nal	âne
ni	mani	nir	mine
né	miné		mène
nou	minou	nour	

COMPRENONS

le nid   la narine   simone mène l'âne

1 <u>ne</u>* mords pas la mine !
2 ne donne pas de limonade à mina !

* à présenter globalement

CTURE EXPRESSIVE

1 simone a chaud, elle est malade.

2 elle demande de la limonade.

3 nicolas donne de la limonade à la malade.

4 mémé donne la poule à simone, elle rit.

5 *voilà le nid de la poule.*

6 *la poule dort sur le nid.*

7 *nicolas ne donne pas de limonade à mémé.*

CTURE COURANTE

Un matin, Nicolas dit à l'âne : « Donne-moi ton nez.

— Pour quoi faire ? — Pour faire du cinéma. »

Et Nicolas met le nez de l'âne.

Nicolas va chez la poule : « Gloussette, mon amie, donne-moi ton nid.

— Pour quoi faire ? — Pour faire du cinéma. »

Et Nicolas prend le nid de la poule.

Nicolas connaît aussi un canard : « Petit canard jaune, donne-moi tes pattes.

— Pour quoi faire ? — Pour faire du cinéma. »

Et Nicolas nage avec les pattes du canard.

Nicolas continue… Maintenant, il a les nattes de Mina, le bonnet de Simone et la canne de pépé.

Ne riez pas, notre Nicolas fait du cinéma.

CTÉE

1 Nicolas regarde la télé — 2 Il rit — 3 L'âne va à l'école — 4 La poule boit de la limonade.

monique apporte la pipe pour papa

monique apporte la pipe pour papa

ap	porte		pipe		pour		papa
p	p		p	p		p		p	p
↑	↑		↑	↑		↑		↑	↑

pa	**pour**	**pipe**	
pi	pir	pipe	pile
po	pore	pope	pole
pou	pour	poupe	poule
pa	par	pape	pale
pé	père	pépé	pèle

      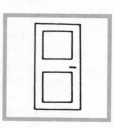   

le pot   la pomme   la porte   le repas

1 médor porte le sac de papa.
2 où va papa ? il part pour Paris.
3 la poule est derrière la porte.
4 voilà le pot pour le repas.
5 pépé apporte <u>une</u>* poupée pour monique.

* à présenter globalement.

1 le papa de monique apporte une poupée.
2 il porte la poupée sur le lit.
3 maman, où est le pot pour le repas?
4 où est ma pomme pour l'école?
5 la pomme n'est pas pour l'école,
6 elle est pour le repas.
7 *voilà une souris pour le repas de minet.*
8 *médor, apporte le sac pour papa.*
9 *papa part pour paris.*

Le premier jour de l'an, papa demande à pépé, à mémé et à ses amis Paul, Pierre et Paméla de venir dîner à la maison. C'est un grand repas.

Maman prépare des petits poissons, papa découpe un poulet, Jean apporte un grand plat pour les petits pois, Monique prend des pommes, des poires, des bananes et des oranges pour faire une salade de fruits.

Ce jour-là, il n'y a pas de soupe, mais un bon pâté de lapin. Ah! Quel repas! Après le repas, tout le monde va au jardin pour prendre le café. « N'oublie pas ta pipe, papa. »

1 Elle part pour Paris — 2 Elle mord dans la pomme — 3 La pipe de papa est dans le sac de maman.

14

qui tire une pelote sur le tapis ?

qui tire une pelote sur le tapis ?

tire		pe	lote		ta	pi
t			t			t
t			*t*			*t*

PRONONÇONS

ta	**tire**	**lote**	**tate**
to	tor	rote	mate
tou	tour	route	latte
ti	tir	rite	natte
ta	tar	rate	patte

COMPRENONS

une patte   une natte   une moto   une tomate

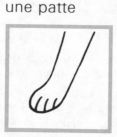   

une toupie   une tête   une tarte   une tartine

1 la patte de minet.
2 il tape à la porte.
3 tourne la tête !

4 tourne, petite toupie !
5 la moto roule sur la rout
6 ta poupée a une natte.

CTURE EXPRESSIVE

1 qui tape à la porte ? c'est simone.
2 qui est à côté de la télé ? c'est mémé.
3 simone apporte une tarte.
4 c'est une tarte pour mémé.
5 qui est sur le tapis ? c'est minet.
6 tourne la tête mémé, regarde, il tire la pelote.
7 ne tire pas ma pelote, petit chat.
8 *la moto tourne sur la route.*
9 *qui tape le tapis ? c'est maman.*
10 *la toupie tourne sur la télé.*

CTURE COURANTE

Madame Tartine est toujours en retard.
Elle court chez le pâtissier pour acheter une boîte de petits gâteaux.
Vite, elle traverse la rue, elle monte dans un autobus, elle tourne autour des maisons, elle tape à une porte : toc ! toc ! toc ! et elle entre.
« C'est Madame Tartine ! J'apporte des gâteaux pour le goûter. — Merci, Madame Tartine. Voulez-vous une tasse de thé avec une petite tarte aux pommes ? Attendez, voilà, je tire la table sur le tapis, à côté de vous. »

CTÉE

1 Nicolas joue avec la toupie — 2 Il est sur la moto — 3 Jacques tape l'âne — 4 C'est mal — 5 La poupée a une natte.

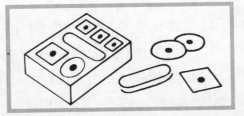 

1 ni - na - né - nou - no - la - le - li - lo - lé

2 ma - mi - mé - mou - mo

3 tou - ta - tar - to - ti - té

4 po - por - pi - pé - pa - pou

5 *le nid - la pomme - la toupie - la moto*

6 *la pelote - l'âne - la tomate - la mine*

7 *la limonade - la patte - la porte - la tartine*

mor → **n**or		po**r** → po**l**		**t**or → ro**te**	
mar	nar	par	pal	tar	rate
mir	nir	pir	pil	tir	rite
mour	nour	pour	poul	tour	rout
mal	nal			tal	roule

madame souris va à Paris.

elle porte le sac sur la tête.

elle roule à moto sur la route.

ro, ré, ri, madame souris rit.

lo, lé, lit, elle n'est pas polie.

ro, ré, rou, elle va sur la route.

mol, mil, mal, elle dort sur la malle.

donne la pomme, simone.
dors petite poupée, il est tard.
donne ta patte, médor.
apporte le sac pour papa.

CTURE COURANTE

Je vous présente les amis de papa.

Pierre est professeur. Il est grand, il a une tête carrée, une barbe noire, de petites lunettes au bout de son nez.

Tous les matins, il prend l'autobus pour aller à l'école. Le dimanche, il va à la pêche avec papa.

Paul est dans un garage. Il répare les voitures, les motos et même des bateaux à moteur.

Il est petit. Il porte toujours des bottes jaunes, il parle vite, il court toujours, il rit, il est très amusant. Il est le mari de Paméla.

Paméla est une belle dame, mais elle est petite comme son mari. Elle fait des chapeaux pour les dames; de jolis chapeaux de toutes les couleurs.

TÉE

1 La souris dort sur la malle — 2 Le chat lève sa patte — 3 Voilà Médor — 4 Minet va sous le lit — 5 Mini la petite souris rit.

regarde papa, un chat sur le lit, tape-le

regarde papa, un chat sur le lit, tape-le

re	garde		le		tape	le

re   le   le

e   **e**

e   *e*

PRONONÇONS

le   le chat
re   regarde papa
me   il me regarde
pe   petit père, tape-le
ne   ne regarde pas
te   il te regarde

COMPRENONS

une petite robe   un petit chat

une petite poupée   un petit nid

1 minet mord la tarte.
2 jacques, simone te parle !
3 la toupie, monique, elle tourne ?

URE EXPRESSIVE

1 voilà le chat, papa, tape-le !

2 voilà l'âne de simone. papa, regarde-le !

3 voilà le sac de papa. médor, apporte-le !

4 le lit, maman. tire-le !

5 *le pot, jacques. répare-le !*

6 *simone, c'est jacques. il te regarde ?*

7 *oui. il me regarde.*

URE COURANTE

Petit chaperon rouge est une petite fille qui porte toujours un bonnet rouge sur la tête. Un jour, sa maman lui dit :

« Grand-mère est malade. Voilà un panier avec un petit pot de beurre et une galette pour elle. Va !... mais, fais vite. Ne t'arrête pas, ne regarde pas les arbres ni les bêtes, ne parle à personne, n'ouvre pas le pot de beurre et ne mange pas la galette. — Non maman ! »

Mais le petit chaperon rouge n'écoute pas sa mère. Un lapin passe... Elle s'arrête. Il court derrière un arbre... Elle le regarde.

Maintenant le loup est devant elle :

« Où vas-tu petit chaperon rouge ? — Je vais chez ma grand-mère... »

Vous connaissez la fin.

ÉE

1 Il te regarde — 2 Ne le tape pas — 3 Elle me parle — 4 Ne la tire pas — 5 Simone, répare-le.

simone, passe la soupe !

simone, passe la soupe !

si	mone

s

ⱴ

la	soupe

s

ⱴ

pass

ss

ⱴⱴ

si
sa
sou
si
so
se

elle sale
la souris
le sirop
il sort
il se roule

passe
tasse
pousse
lisse
l'os

simone sale la soupe

la souris sort de la tasse

il est assis, il a un os

il se roule, il se salit, il est s

1 voilà le sirop pour le malade.
2 un os sur le lit ! sors, médor !

URE EXPRESSIVE

1 simone, passe la soupe, ne te salis pas ! passe la tasse !

2 voilà une tasse de soupe pour simone.

3 la tasse roule sur le tapis, voilà de la soupe sur la robe
de simone, sur le tapis, c'est sale.

4 voilà un os pour médor, c'est l'os de médor.

5 assis médor ! voilà un os.

6 *médor est assis, il a l'os sous sa patte.
minet passe, il va sur le sac, il regarde l'os.*

7 *médor ne donne pas l'os, alors, minet sort.*

URE COURANTE

Monsieur Saunier se lève tous les matins à 6 heures. Il passe dans la salle
de bains et il se lave. Dans la salle à manger, il s'assoit pour prendre son
petit déjeuner : une tasse de café sans sucre et une tartine de beurre salé.
Il met ses chaussures, sa veste, son chapeau. Il prend son sac et il s'en va.
Il attend l'autobus devant la poste.
Ce matin, l'autobus ne passe pas. Alors Monsieur Saunier sort sa grosse moto.
Mais elle ne veut pas partir : elle tousse, elle saute et elle s'arrête.
Bonne journée Monsieur Saunier !

ÉE

1 Simone sale une tasse de soupe — 2 Médor est assis, un os sous sa
patte — 3 De la soupe sur le tapis : c'est sale !

écoute, le car passe à côté de l'école

écoute, le car passe à côté de l'école

é	coute

car

cô	té

l'é	col

c   c   c   c

c   c   c   c

PRONONÇONS

co   **car**

co	cor	la colle	soc	toc	r
cou	cour	il coule	sic	tic	p
ca	car	il casse	sac	tac	l

c = k   kilo - ki - ko - ka - ké.

COMPRENONS

qui porte le sac ?   un kilo de carottes

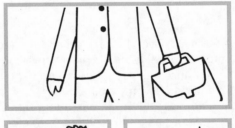

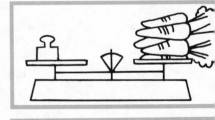

un coq   tic, tac   elle coupe la tarte

1 nicolas casse la tasse.
2 le camarade de jacques copie.
3 le canard court.
4 la cour de l'école.

CTURE EXPRESSIVE

1 qui coupe la tarte ? c'est maman.
2 qui casse la tasse ? c'est nicolas.
3 qui est nicolas ? c'est le camarade de jacques.
4 cours à l'école, jacques, il est tard, le car passe.
5 jacques est à l'école. Il copie le mot kilo, il coupe un carré.
6 *cocorico ! écoute le coq. cot ! cot ! cot ! écoute la poule.*
7 *coucou ! qui est là ? c'est nicolas.*

CTURE COURANTE

« Bonjour Nicolas ! Viens avec moi chez Colette. Comment ? tu tournes la tête ? tu te sauves dans l'arbre ?
— Qu'est-ce que tu as ?
— Qu'est-ce que tu fais dans cet arbre ?
— Cocorico ! Ah ! le coq est avec toi !
— Coin, coin, coin !... Le canard aussi ! »

« Nicolas ! Qu'est-ce que tu caches à côté de toi ? Mais c'est le cartable de Jacques !
— Qu'est-ce qu'il y a dans ce cartable ?
— Il y a un kilo de sucre, du chocolat et des carottes : c'est un cadeau pour mes camarades, répond Nicolas. Ils sont très contents. »

CTÉE

1 Dans le sac de Maman — 2 il y a un kilo de carottes — 3 un coq, un canard — 4 Écoute, voilà le car qui passe.

médor demande un os

médor demande un os

dor

d

d

de	mande

d   d

d   d

de		**dor**	**mand**
do	le dos	dar	moc
da	madame	dir	rac
di	midi	dour	rio
dou	c'est doux		coud
dé			

donne ta patte à la dame !   il dort sur le dos

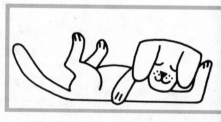

le dos du chat est doux.   le coude de monique.

il est midi.

CTURE EXPRESSIVE

1 une dame passe, elle a un os <u>dans</u>* le sac,
médor court derrière elle, il demande l'os,
la dame donne l'os à médor.
donne ta patte à la dame, médor !

2 dodo ! ma petite poupée.
monique dit à sa poupée de dormir.

3 *simone est malade, elle a mal dans le dos. maman
ne donne pas de limonade, elle donne le sirop à la
malade. à midi, madame michaud apporte le repas.*

CTURE COURANTE

Il est deux heures et demie.
Assis devant la porte de l'école, Monsieur le Directeur s'endort.
C'est dimanche. La grande cour est vide. Aujourd'hui, pas de devoirs, pas de
professeurs, pas d'élèves ! Les grands arbres du jardin regardent Monsieur le
Directeur dormir.
Pan ! dans le dos ! Monsieur le Directeur saute sur sa chaise : « Qu'est-ce
que c'est ? » C'est un ballon.
Pan ! sur le nez. C'est une tomate.
Pan ! sur la tête. C'est une carotte.
Vite, Nicolas descend du toit de la maison et il se sauve derrière l'école.
« Tu ris Nicolas, mais ton ballon est perdu. »

PRONONÇONS

Groupes avec accent tonique

c'est un sac ? donne-le !   non, il ne regarde pas.
c'est un canard ? attrape-le !   non, il ne roule pas.
c'est un coq ? écoute-le !   non, il ne copie pas.
c'est un carré ? dessine-le !   non, il ne tourne pas.
c'est un os ? apporte-le !   non, il ne passe pas.

1 da - de - dou - di - do - dé.
2 si - sa - so - sou - sé - se.
3 ca - co - cou.
4 voilà la tasse de nicolas - ne la casse pas !
5 c'est l'os de médor - ne le donne pas !
6 voilà le sac de la dame - ne le salis pas !
7 *ne cours pas dans la cour de l'école !*
8 *ne passe pas à côté de nicolas.*

LECTURE EXPRESSIVE

1 nicolas porte le pot de maman sur sa tête.
2 il tourne, tourne sur le tapis.
3 écoute, voilà maman.
4 nicolas court derrière la porte.

5 crac ! le pot est cassé.

6 qui a cassé le pot ? demande maman.

7 *c'est médor ! dit nicolas.*

8 *papa tape nicolas - il répare le pot cassé.*

LECTURE COURANTE

Dans le grand arbre, derrière notre maison, il y a un nid.

Un petit nid, rond et chaud.

Simone me dit : « Il est vide, ce nid, va le prendre !

— Non, il n'est pas vide, regarde les becs jaunes qui sortent. Il y a des petits dedans.

— Il y en a combien ?

— Je ne sais pas.

— Où est la mère ? Elle se cache ?

— Non, elle ne se cache pas ; écoute-la siffler : « sri ! sri ! ». Elle a peur pour ses enfants.

— Voilà le père. Il n'est pas content. Regarde-le passer au-dessus de nos têtes !

— C'est assez Simone, partons. »

regarde dans la boîte, bébé, il y a une balle

regarde dans la boîte, bébé, il y a une balle

boîte		**bé**	**bé**		**balle**
b		b	b		b
ℓ		*ℓ*	*ℓ*		*ℓ*

---

bé

bo	bol	**une boîte**	
bo	bol	une botte	robe
bou	bour	une boule	
ba	bal	une balle	barbe
bi	bir	la bile	

debout médor !   la belle barbe   une botte   un bol

il y a une petite bête
dans le bol

la boule roule
sur le bord de la boîte

1 où est la petite bête ?
2 la bête est là-bas, dans une boîte.
3 où est ma balle ?
4 ta balle est sur le bord de la télé.

ECTURE EXPRESSIVE

1. papa apporte une belle boîte pour monique.
2. écoute, il y a une bête dans la boîte.
3. non*, regarde, c'est une belle robe.
4. il y a une petite balle pour Jean.
5. pépé coupe sa barbe.
6. où est nicolas? il est là-bas, debout sur le bord de la route.
7. il a mis un bol sur sa tête. comme il est bête.

ECTURE COURANTE

« Tu vois là-bas, ce garçon avec une belle bicyclette bleue. Eh bien, c'est Barnabé. Barnabé est un camarade de Jean
C'est un beau garçon, grand et fort, toujours bien habillé. Regarde son beau blouson noir et ses belles bottes rouges.
— Bien sûr, son père est riche. C'est le boulanger de la rue du chat botté.
— Ah ! il habite rue du chat botté ! Je le connais ce Barnabé.
Il a beaucoup d'amis.
— Bien sûr, il joue bien au ballon et aux billes et... il a toujours les poches pleines de bonbons. »

DICTÉE

1 Il y a une balle dans la boîte de bébé — 2 La poupée a une belle robe —
3 Nicolas tire sur la barbe de pépé — 4 Il est bête.

**nicolas mange une orange,
il en donne à maman**

nicolas mange une orange, il en donne à maman

mange		o	range		en		ma	man
an			**an**		**en**			**an**
an			*an*		*en*			*an*

man - nan - lan - ran - pan - ban - tan - dan - can
sen - pen - ten - den - men - nen - len - ren.
pente - sente - tante - lente - mante - rente.
lampe - rampe - tempe - tambour - il emporte.

elle danse rapidement

elle danse lentement

le tambour est sur le banc

bébé a une dent

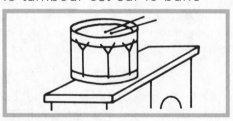

il mange une orange

il s'endort

la belle lampe

CTURE EXPRESSIVE

1 pan ! pan ! rataplan ! écoute, c'est nicolas assis sur le banc.
2 il tape sur le tambour lentement, rapidement.
3 monique l'entend, elle danse en même temps.
4 voilà une orange, ne la mange pas nicolas, range-la dans la boîte. va-t'en ! nicolas s'en va.
5 *comment va mémé ? elle va mal.*

CTURE COURANTE

Les vacances commencent dimanche. Quelle chance ! Depuis vendredi, les enfants attendent ce moment. « Encore deux jours, et c'est fini ! »
On danse au son du tambour. On entend rire et chanter dans toutes les maisons.
« Nous allons chez tante Martine à la campagne trala la la ! »
« Jean, n'oublie pas d'emporter ton manteau. »
« Henri, range tes médicaments dans la grande valise. Tu as encore mal au ventre. Il faut en prendre. »
« Monique, demande de l'argent à maman. Il faut cent trente francs pour les places du car. »
Maman descend de la chambre :
« Silence, les enfants ! bébé s'endort. Soyez gentils, parlez doucement. »

ICTÉE

1 Elle danse au son du tambour — 2 Bébé s'endort — 3 Nicolas mange une orange — 4 Il s'est cassé une dent.

| **une voiture roule dans la rue du petit solda** |

une voiture roule dans la rue du petit soldat

une		**voi**	**ture**		**rue**		**d**
u			u		u		u
u			*u*		*u*		*u*

PRONONÇONS

rue   **ture**

du	tordu	dur		tou	–	ti	–	t
tu	tortue	rature		sou	–	si	–	s
mu	ému	mur		pou	–	pi	–	p
lu	il a lu	lune		rou	–	ri	–	r
su	tissu	sur		bou	–	bi	–	b
				nou	–	ni	–	n

line - lune
boule - bile - bulle - moule - mille - mule

COMPRENONS

il court sur le mur   la tortue   la lune

1 voilà du tissu pour une robe.
2 l'école est dans la rue du petit soldat.
3 tu lis le numéro sur le mur ? il y a 8.
4 la tortue a un ruban <u>et</u>* une culotte, c'est amusant.

CTURE EXPRESSIVE

1 il y a une belle voiture dans la rue.

2 où est-elle ? dans la rue du chat ?

3 non, elle roule dans la rue du petit soldat.

4 lis le numéro de la voiture : 12.06.

5 où cours-tu petite tortue ?
sur le mur, sur le mur.
où vas-tu ? sur la lune, sur la lune.
une tortue sur la lune, c'est amusant.

CTURE COURANTE

Le lapin dit un jour à la tortue : « Je cours plus vite que toi.

— Ce n'est pas sûr, répond la tortue.

— Alors nous allons faire une course.

— C'est entendu, dit la tortue. Le départ est ici et l'arrivée là-bas, près du mur. Attention : un, deux, trois, partez ! »

Le lapin court vite, il est sûr de gagner. Alors, il s'arrête pour manger et s'endort sur le dos. Dame tortue, elle, continue lentement, mais sûrement.

Monsieur lapin se réveille :

« Mais, qu'est-ce que c'est là-bas, près du mur ? Mais c'est dame tortue qui arrive ! courons vite, vite.

— Trop tard monsieur lapin, dit la tortue, je suis arrivée la première. »

Courir vite, c'est bien ; mais il ne faut pas s'arrêter en chemin.

ICTÉE

1 A midi, il a bu du coca-cola — 2 Où est la rue de la Lune ? — 3 A côté de la rue de la Tortue — 4 C'est amusant.

jacques, ne fume pas !
ce n'est pas pour les enfants

jacques ne fume pas ! ce n'est pas pour les enfan

| **fume** | | **en** | **fants** |

f   f

f   *f*

PRONONÇONS

fan		**enfant**
fi	fil	il finit
fa	fade	la farine
fu	fume	la fumée
fou	four	la fourmi
fo	fort	la folle
fé	fée	café
fan - fen		enfant

COMPRENONS

il fume la pipe la fumée   il finit sa tasse de café

la fourmi   les fourmis   l'enfant   les enfants

1 un sac de farine — une bobine de fil.
2 il est fort - il est fou - elle est folle.

1 il y a de la fumée dans la voiture.
2 c'est jacques qui fume la pipe.
3 il est fou ! ce n'est pas pour les enfants !
4 *maman, tu as fini le café ?*
5 *oui, regarde, il fume dans les bols.*

Mademoiselle cigale est une petite bête un peu folle. Quand il fait beau, elle joue de la flûte dans les rues, dans les cafés, dans les cours. Au son de la flûte, toutes les fenêtres s'ouvrent. On écoute la musique, on est content ; alors, on jette deux ou trois francs à la chanteuse.

Pour Mademoiselle cigale, c'est la fête tous les jours. Chez elle, il y a des fleurs partout. A ses amis, elle offre toujours les plus beaux fruits et leur fait des gâteaux avec la farine la plus fine.

Mais, une personne n'aime pas Mademoiselle cigale : c'est Madame la fourmi. Madame la fourmi est une petite bête très sage. Sa maison est toujours bien rangée, bien lavée, bien fermée. Elle n'a pas le temps de chanter ou de faire des gâteaux. Quand elle achète du sucre, du café ou de la farine, c'est pour elle, ce n'est pas pour les autres.

Il n'y a jamais de fleurs dans sa maison : c'est trop cher. Quand il fait froid, elle fait du feu et quand Mademoiselle cigale frappe à sa porte, elle n'ouvre pas.

1 Il y a une bête sur le fil — 2 Oui, c'est une fourmi — 3 Papa fume — 4 Le café aussi.

PRONONÇONS

Groupes avec accent tonique

Oppositions de syllabes

pi	pou	pu
bi	bou	bu
fi	fou	fu
pir	pour	pur
bir	bour	bur
fir	four	fur

sous le petit bureau.
elle coupe un petit ruban.
il court sur le petit mur
où est le numéro dix ?
c'est du tissu rouge.

1 be - bou - bi - bu - bo - bé - ba - ban.

2 fo - fa - fan - fe - fé - fi - fou - fu.

3 les bols - le café - la farine - les belles robes.

4 les enfants - les dents - le banc -
le médicament.

5 *la belle balle - les fourmis - la tortue - la lun*

6 *les numéros - la barbe - le tissu.*

LECTURE EXPRESSIVE

1 où vas-tu belle tortue ? dans la rue ?

2 ce n'est pas pour les tortues !

3 si tu vas dans la rue, tu rouleras sous le
voitures.

4 regarde le nid de fourmis, maman !

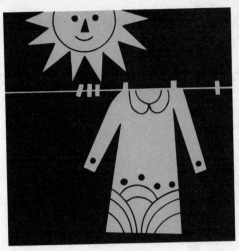 

5 en voilà une qui court, une qui danse, une qui mange, et une qui porte une petite bête sur son dos. elle est forte !

6 *il y a une robe sur le fil.*

7 *ce n'est pas ta robe, monique ?*

8 *si, c'est ma robe.*

Bubu est un enfant gentil, mais il n'est pas très intelligent.

Un jour sa maman lui dit :

« Va porter ce gâteau à tante Babette. Fais attention, prends-le bien, ne le laisse pas tomber. »

— « Oui, maman. »

Bubu met le gâteau dans une boîte, il serre fort la boîte dans ses bras et il s'en va...

Quand il arrive chez sa tante, le gâteau est comme de la farine.

« Bubu, tu es bête ! on porte les gâteaux sur la tête. »

Un autre jour, sa maman lui dit de porter du beurre à sa tante Babette. Alors Bubu met le beurre sur sa tête. Mais il fait très chaud.

Quand il arrive, le beurre n'est plus sur sa tête, il est sur sa figure, sur son manteau, sur sa culotte et même sur ses chaussures !

« Bubu, tu es bête ! On met le beurre dans un pot avec de l'eau froide. »

papa arrive avec sa valise

papa arrive avec sa valise

ar	rive

v

ʋ

a	vec

v

ʋ

va	lis

v

ʋ

va   **avec**

vi   vide   il va vite   **riv**
vou   voûte   il vous parle   arriʋ
va   va-t'en   lavabo   couʋ
vé   vélo   lavé   laʋ
                                              élèʋ

fo - vo - fe - ve - fu - vu - fan - van - fen - ven

elle se lave devant le lavabo   il vole   un élève

1 il a vu - venir - le vent.
2 voilà une boîte vide.
3 monique vous parle de sa poupée.
4 il s'en va à la ville.
5 le vélo va vite.
6 ne va pas devant le vélo, va-t'en !
7 l'élève range son sac avant de sortir.

CTURE EXPRESSIVE

1 papa va venir. oui, le voilà !
2 il arrive de la ville. il est à vélo. il roule vite.
3 *il arrive avec une valise. il y a du tissu dedans.*
4 *médor court devant le vélo. va-t'en, médor !*

CTURE COURANTE

Un autre jour, sa maman veut offrir un petit chat à tante Babette.
« Bubu, viens ici, voilà un petit chat, va le donner à tante Babette. — Oui, maman. »
Bubu met le chat dans le pot avec de l'eau froide, il prend son vélo et il s'en va... Quand il arrive devant sa tante, il ouvre vite le pot : la pauvre bête est malade, elle va mourir. « Bubu, tu es trop bête ! » On met le chat par terre ; on le mène avec une ficelle autour du cou.
Vingt jours plus tard, sa maman lui dit :
« Voilà un livre, va l'apporter à tante Babette. — Oui, maman. »
Bubu met le livre par terre, il met une ficelle autour et il le mène comme on mène un petit chat.
Quand il arrive, qu'est-ce qu'il y a au bout de la ficelle ?
Un livre ? Non ! Une chèvre !
« Où est mon livre ? demande tante Babette.
— Dans le ventre de la chèvre ! répond Bubu.
— Ah ! Bubu, sauve-toi vite ! Je ne veux plus te voir. »

ICTÉE

1 La valise est vide — 2 Le vélo roule vite — 3 Le car va vite — 4 Elle lave le chat dans le lavabo.

où sont les bonbons ?

où sont les bonbons ?

sont
on
on

bon	bons
on	**on**
on	*on*

PRONONÇONS

ton	**ton lit**	**bouton**
mon	monte	simon
lon	l'onde	ballon
ron	ronde	marron
fon	fondu	ils font

von - don - non - pon - bon - con - son

van - dan - nan - pan - ban - can - san

son - sonne - simon - simone - bon - bonne

COMPRENONS

des boutons   des marrons   le pont   du savon

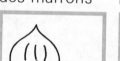

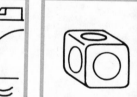

il monte sur son vélo   il tombe   un pantalon

1 ils ont de la confiture. c'est bon !

2 ils sont contents, ils font les fous — dansons la ronde !

27

LECTURE EXPRESSIVE

1 les enfants sont à l'école.
2 ils ont lu, ils ont écouté et ils ont fait du calcul.
3 alors la dame donne des bonbons.
4 ils sont contents.
5 *ils vont dans la cour avec le ballon.*
6 *dansons la ronde et courons sur le pont.*

LECTURE COURANTE

Jean et Henri sont en vacances à la campagne. Ils sont très contents. On est bien chez l'oncle Simon !

Le matin, les garçons se lavent à la fontaine avec du savon.

Ils mettent un vieux pantalon, un blouson et après un bon petit déjeuner, ils sortent de la maison.

« Vite, Jean, allons près du pont. Il y a beaucoup de moutons. Nous allons jouer à saute-mouton. »

Mais Jean aime mieux regarder dans l'eau sous le pont : il y a de gros poissons. Il dit à Henri :

« Prenons de longs bâtons et avec un fil, pêchons-les.

— Mais nous n'avons pas de fil !

— Alors jouons au ballon ! »

Henri préfère monter sur un arbre. En haut de l'arbre, il y a des marrons.

« Attention Henri, ne tombe pas ! »

DICTÉE

1 Les bonbons sont bons — 2 L'orange est bonne — 3 Les enfants font la ronde — 4 Elle se lave avec du savon.

2

l'auto tombe au fond de l'eau

l'auto tombe au fond de l'eau

au	to

au

au

au

au

au

l'eau

eau

eau

PRONONÇONS

au	**l'eau**		
bau	beau	corbeau	au bord
sau	seau	il saute	aussi
tau	teau	couteau	autobus
fau		il faut	au fond

pau - rau - lau - mau - nau - cau - dau - vau

COMPRENONS

elle saute
à la corde   un manteau   un couteau   un bureau

1 le bateau va sur l'eau.
2 l'auto roule au bord de l'eau.
3 papa va au bureau en autobus. henri aussi.
4 il faut un manteau pour sortir.
5 il aura un cadeau, un beau couteau et beaucoup de
   bonbons.

TURE EXPRESSIVE

1 une auto arrive vite.
2 la voilà au bord de l'eau.
3 <u>plouf</u>* elle tombe dans l'eau.
4 il y a beaucoup d'eau.
5 l'auto est au fond.
6 il faut la sortir vite.
7 *un beau bateau passe par là.*
8 *ohé bateau ! il y a une auto au fond de l'eau.*

CTURE COURANTE

1 Une auto
   Sur le bord du ruisseau
   Le chauffeur s'endort
   Et l'auto tombe à l'eau.

2 Quand le chauffeur sort de l'eau
   Il n'a plus de chapeau !
   Quand l'auto sort de l'eau
   Elle n'a plus de capot
   Elle est en morceaux...

3 Où est le chapeau ?
   Où est le capot ?
   Où sont les morceaux ?
   Dans l'eau, dans l'eau du ruisseau.

4 Non, non, non dit l'oiseau
   Moi, je sais où est le chapeau
   Dis vite, dis vite !
   Dans un arbre, dans un arbre,
   C'est un nid pour mes petits.

CTÉE

1 Un joli bateau va sur l'eau du lavabo — 2 L'auto de Papa roule vite —
3 Maman a un beau manteau — 4 et Papa une belle auto.

nicolas goûte le gâteau de grand-mère

nicolas goûte le gâteau de grand-mère

goûte
g
g

gâ	teau
g	
g	

grand-	mèr
g	
g	

gâ

ga   gar   **goûte**

go   gor   gare   regarde
gou   gour   gomme   fagot
                   goutte   il goûte

gan - gon - gau - gu - grand

des gouttes
d'eau

des gants

des légumes

la figure

1 voilà un grand gâteau pour les enfants.
2 ils sont gâtés.
3 nicolas garde le gâteau.
4 il le goûte, il est gourmand.
5 grand-père va à la gare.

1 grand-mère apporte un grand gâteau.
2 c'est un beau gâteau pour le repas des enfants.
3 comme ils sont gâtés !
4 nicolas arrive, il regarde si grand-mère est partie.

5 il goûte tout : la soupe, les légumes, le gâteau.

6 comme il est gourmand !

7 voilà grand-mère.

8 *nicolas a du gâteau sur la figure, il sera puni.*

9 *grand-père apporte un cadeau pour grand-mère.*

LECTURE COURANTE

Elle part dans le matin gris, quand le coq chante. Elle porte ses légumes au marché. Regardez sa bonne figure ronde.

Elle met toujours un gros manteau vert, de grosses chaussures jaunes et des gants rouges. Elle porte son grand panier sur sa tête.

Cette marchande n'a pas de magasin.

Tous les mercredis et les jeudis, elle vient de la campagne avec ses choux, ses salades et ses carottes. Elle crie :

« Regardez les belles salades, les radis ! Achetez mes beaux légumes ! »

La grenouille

La petite grenouille verte est froide dans la main.

Ne la gardez pas serrée.

Ouvrez la main et regardez-la :

Ses yeux sont deux gouttes d'or.

Elle regarde à droite, à gauche, et... hop ! elle saute !...

DICTÉE

1 Elle goûte la soupe — 2 Une goutte d'eau tombe dans le lavabo — 3 Un chapeau et des gants — 4 C'est beau.

LECTURE EXPRESSIVE

1 vé - vi - vou - vu - va - van - vo - von - ven - va

2 gou - gu - go - gon - ga - gan - gau.

3 ron - lon - mon - non - fon - von - ton - sc

4 pau - beau - fau - veau - tau - seau.

1 où sont les enfants de madame michaud

2 ils sont dans l'autobus, ils vont à l'éco

3 où sont les gommes ?

4 elles sont sur le bureau.

5 les bons élèves ne font pas de fautes.

6 *il ne faut pas de gomme pour le bon élève*

7 *les parents de jacques ont un bateau.*

LECTURE COURANTE

Oncle Simon, raconte-nous une histoire amusante.

« Voilà, un matin, je mène mes moutons aux champs. Je passe sur le gr
pont qui traverse la rivière et je vois un homme assis au bord de l'eau. C
drôle ! il a un journal dans sa main gauche et un marteau dans l'autre m
Je vais le voir et je demande :

— Pardon monsieur, qu'est-ce que vous faites ?

— Chut ! je pêche.

— Vous pêchez avec un journal et un marteau ?

— Mais oui, regardez : je tiens mon journal au-dessus de l'eau, les poiss
viennent le lire. Ils sortent la tête, alors, avec mon marteau, je les frappe
je les prends.

— Et... vous en prenez beaucoup ?

— Oui monsieur, vous êtes le onzième ! »

Imprimé en France, par l'Imprimerie Hérissey, Évreux (Eure) - N° 51698 - Dépôt légal : N° 8698-07-1990 - Collection n° 16 - Édition ■

15/2991/6